JUST ENOUGH

UNIX

PAUL K. ANDERSEN

PURDUE UNIVERSITY

WCB Wm. C. Brown Publishers

Dubuque, Iowa•Melbourne, Australia•Oxford, England

Book Team

Editor *Earl McPeek*
Developmental Editor *Linda M. Meehan*
Production Editor *Anne E. Scroggin*

Wm. C. Brown Publishers
A Division of Wm. C. Brown Communications, Inc.

Vice President and General Manager *George Bergquist*
National Sales Manager *Vincent R. Di Blasi*
Assistant Vice President, Editor-in-Chief *Edward G. Jaffe*
Marketing Manager *Elizabeth Robbins*
Advertising Manager *Amy Schmitz*
Managing Editor, Production *Colleen A. Yonda*
Manager of Visuals and Design *Faye M. Schilling*

Publishing Services Manager *Karen J. Slaght*
Permissions/Records Manager *Connie Allendorf*

Wm. C. Brown Communications, Inc.

Chairman Emeritus *Wm. C. Brown*
Chairman and Chief Executive Officer *Mark C. Falb*
President and Chief Operating Officer *G. Franklin Lewis*
Corporate Vice President, Operations *Beverly Kolz*
Corporate Vice President, President of WCB Manufacturing *Roger Meyer*

Library of Congress Catalog Card Number: 92–73659

ISBN 0–697–13172–6

Printed in the United States of America by Wm. C. Brown Communications, Inc.,
2460 Kerper Boulevard, Dubuque, IA 52001

10 9 8 7 6 5 4 3 2 1

To Ginger.

Table of Contents

Preface

What is UNIX?

Mention computers, and most people tend to think of computer *hardware*—the physical device, consisting of circuit boards, a central processing unit (CPU), memory chips, etc. Equally important, however, is the *software*—the programs that tell the hardware what to do. Without software, a computer is just a box with wires attached to it.

An *operating system* is an important kind of software that manages the resources of the computer. You might think of the operating system as the master control program for the entire computer system, hardware and software.

In this book you will learn about the UNIX operating system. UNIX is fast becoming the standard computer operating system in industry, government, and education. It is especially popular in academia: according to AT&T, where UNIX was developed, every major university in the United States now has at least one computer system running under UNIX.

Which Version of UNIX?

Although UNIX originated at the AT&T Bell Laboratories, much of its subsequent development has occurred at the University of California, Berkeley. Computer manufacturers, too, have gotten into the act, producing their own variations on the UNIX theme. Examples include AIX, from IBM; A/UX, from Apple Computer; HP-UX, from Hewlett-Packard; SunOS, from Sun Microsystems; ULTRIX, from Digital Equipment Corporation; and XENIX, from Microsoft.

These versions of UNIX are quite similar. Most can trace their ancestry to either AT&T UNIX or Berkeley UNIX; some are amalgams of both. This book presents features that are found on almost all UNIX systems, with special emphasis on those that are common to AT&T System V and Berkeley System Distribution (BSD) 4.3 UNIX.

Who Should Read This Book?

This book is intended for anyone who wants to acquire a working knowledge of UNIX without having to become a UNIX expert. It is especially appropriate for students of science, engineering, or business who are taking their first computer programming course.

What Does This Book Cover?

This book covers the basics of the UNIX operating system. It has eight main parts:

     I.   INTRODUCTION TO UNIX

    II.   THE UNIX FILE SYSTEM

   III.   THE VISUAL EDITOR

   IV.   UNIX COMMUNICATIONS

INTRODUCTION. In Part I, you will find an overview of the UNIX operating system, and you will learn what you will need to start using it.

THE UNIX FILE SYSTEM. UNIX organizes information in collections called *files*. You will learn how to create, name, rename, copy, and delete files in Part II. You will also learn how UNIX keeps track of your files.

THE VISUAL EDITOR. You can create or modify UNIX files using a utility program called an *editor*. The most popular UNIX editor is called **vi** ("vee-eye"), which is discussed in Part III.

UNIX COMMUNICATIONS. One of the most useful utilities is *electronic mail* (or "E-mail"), which allows you to communicate with other users on the system. The UNIX electronic mail utilities **mail** (Berkeley UNIX) and **mailx** (AT&T System V) are discussed in Part IV.

THE UNIX SHELL. The part of UNIX that interprets user commands and passes them on to the computer is called a *shell*. Many different shells have been written for UNIX; the three most prevalent are the **Bourne Shell** (standard on AT&T System V UNIX), the **C Shell** (standard on Berkeley UNIX), and the **Korn Shell**. These shells are considered in Part V.

SHELL SCRIPTS. The UNIX shell is also a sophisticated programming language. A file containing a program for the UNIX shell is called a *shell script*. Shell scripts are described in Part VI.

PROGRAMMING UNDER UNIX. Almost every UNIX system includes the programming languages C and FORTRAN. Most also include Pascal, and your system may have other languages such as BASIC, Lisp, COBOL, etc. UNIX also offers various software tools called *debuggers*, which are used to find errors ("bugs") in programs. UNIX programming is discussed in VII, with emphasis on C, FORTRAN, and Pascal.

DOCUMENT PREPARATION. The UNIX *text formatters* **nroff** and **troff** allow you to produce attractive memos, reports, and other printed documents. The **ms** *macro package* is a collection of predefined formatting instructions that make the formatters much easier to work with. You can include tables and mathematical equations in your reports by using the table formatter **tbl** and the equation formatter **eqn**. These programs are presented in Part VIII.

How to Use This Book

Anyone who is just starting with UNIX should read straight through Parts I, II, III, IV, and V. The remaining parts may be read in any order. If you would like to learn about shell scripts, read Part VI. If you are interested primarily in using UNIX to program in C,

FORTRAN, or Pascal, you should read Part VII. If you want to use UNIX for document preparation you will want to read Part VIII.

Each part of this book begins with a chapter that explains the material without requiring the use of the computer. Other chapters are called "tutorials." These are intended to be read at the computer terminal. You should plan to spend about an hour at the terminal to cover each tutorial.

At the end of each section, you will find some short exercises. Some exercises are intended to be done at the terminal; these are marked with an asterisk (*). To derive the maximum benefit from this text, be sure to work through all of the exercises.

Notation Used in This Book

This book uses **boldface** to refer to UNIX utilities and commands, and ***bold italics*** for file and directory names. Lines that you are supposed to type into the computer, as well as the computer's responses, are shown in this type:

```
This is what you type
This is how the computer responds
```

Acknowledgments

Many persons helped in the preparation of this book. The following reviewers read the manuscript at various stages in its development and provided helpful comments and suggestions:

Eric P. Bloom
Boston University

Joe Hagarty
Raritan Valley Community College

John Carroll
San Diego State University

Vasant G. Honavar
Iowa State University

Richard J. Easton
Indiana State University

Alexander Stoffel
Mayville State University

Charles Frank
Northern Kentucky University

John Slimick
University of Pittsburgh—Bradford

Donald L. Greenwell
Eastern Kentucky University

This book could not have been produced without the invaluable assistance of Dr. M. G. Scarbrough, colleague and friend.

Part I
INTRODUCTION TO UNIX

1. Introduction to UNIX

In this chapter, you will get an overview of UNIX—what it is, how it works, what it can do for you. You'll also learn some necessary computer terminology, and you'll find out what you will need to begin working on the computer.

Computer Hardware

Computers come in a bewildering range of shapes, sizes, and types. Despite their differences, almost all have the following four essential components (see Figure 1.1):

- ***Central processing unit (CPU).*** The CPU performs calculations and manipulates data.

- ***Main memory*** (a.k.a. ***primary memory***, ***internal memory***). This is the place where the CPU looks for instructions and data to process. Main memory is fast but limited in how much it can hold.

- ***Input/Output (I/O) device.*** I/O devices are used to move information to and from the computer. The most common I/O devices are keyboards, video displays, and printers.

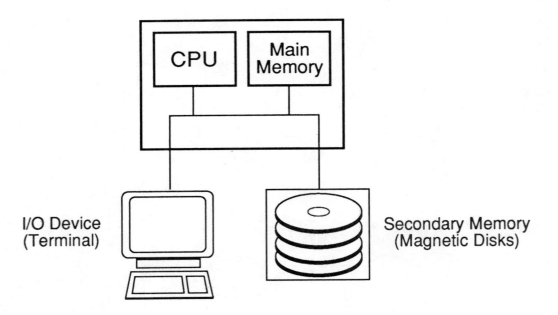

Figure 1.1. A typical computer system. The four parts of a single-user computer are shown. The CPU and main memory are almost always placed together in the same box; the disks and terminal may be separate units.

- *Secondary memory (external memory, mass storage)*. Information that is not immediately needed by the computer is placed in secondary memory. Secondary memory is slower than main memory but can hold much more. The most common secondary storage devices are magnetic disks.

The CPU and the main memory are usually found close together in the same unit; this is what many people mean when they talk of "the computer." Other devices, such as terminals, printers, disk drives, etc., are often called *peripherals*, because they attach to the unit containing the CPU and main memory.

One User or Many?

The computer represented in Figure 1.1 is a *single-user* system. Because it has one terminal, it is able to serve only one person at a time. This is a common arrangement with smaller, *personal* computers.

Large computer systems, on the other hand, often have more power than one person can profitably use. These computers are commonly set up as *multiuser systems,* as depicted in Figure 1.2. Note that the multiuser computer has the same four basic parts as the single-user computer: CPU, main memory, secondary memory, and I/O devices. The main difference is that the multiuser system has multiple I/O devices. (It may also have larger secondary memory.)

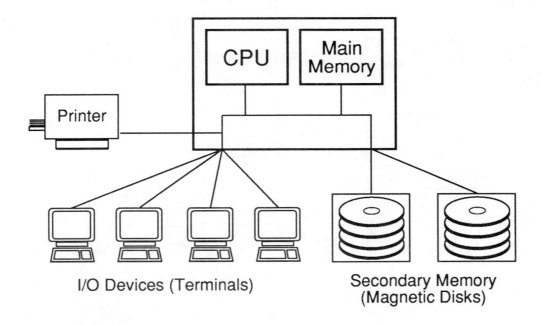

Figure 1.2. A multiuser computer system. This system is set up for four users, who share the CPU, the memory, and other resources such as the printer.

Another way to accommodate multiple users is to link two or more computers together to form a *network*. Figure 1.3 shows a network consisting of three single-user machines (called *hosts* or *workstations*), a printer, and another computer (called a *server*) that has no terminal but does have magnetic disks. In this case, none of the three hosts has its own secondary storage but instead relies on the magnetic disks attached to the server. (The server *serves* the workstations by providing secondary storage for them.)

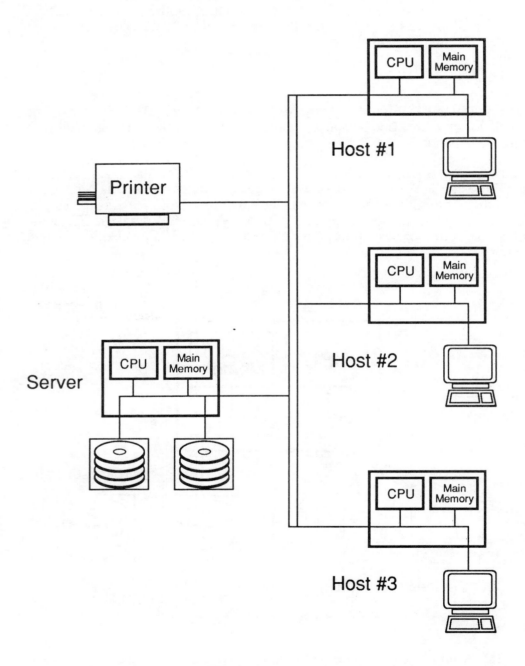

Figure 1.3. A networked computer system. This network includes four computers, one of which is used as a server providing disk storage for the other three.

Operating Systems

As important as the computer hardware is, it can do nothing without *software*, the coded instructions that tell the CPU what to do. An especially important type of software is the *operating system* which performs three vital functions. First, it controls all of the various peripheral devices—printers, disk drives, terminals, and so on—that are attached to the computer. Second, it manages the way other programs are stored and run. And third, it handles communications between the user and the computer, passing commands from the user to the computer, and returning messages from the computer to the user.

Multitasking and Time-Sharing

UNIX is a *multitasking* operating system, meaning that it enables the computer to work on more than one task at a time. The computer can run several of your programs "in background" while you work on another task "in the foreground."

How does the computer do more than one task at a time? The answer is, it doesn't; it only appears to. The computer's CPU is only able to do one thing at a time. However, by switching rapidly back and forth between tasks, performing a little here and a little there, it creates the illusion of being able to do everything at once. This method of working on many different tasks is called *time-sharing*. It is feasible only because (a) the computer is very fast, and (b) UNIX takes care of scheduling what is to be done and when.

UNIX is also a *multiuser* operating system, meaning it can serve more than one person at a time. Again, the computer's CPU can only work on one task at a time, but by switching rapidly back and forth between users, it appears to be interacting with many users simultaneously. Most of the time the computer works so quickly that each user is unaware that the computer is working with anyone else.

Not surprisingly, UNIX can also serve as a single-user operating system for personal computers and workstations. Even as a single-user operating system, however, UNIX retains its multitasking ability.

Versions of UNIX

The two most widely used versions of UNIX are AT&T System V UNIX and Berkeley Software Distribution (BSD) UNIX. Many computer manufacturers offer their own versions of UNIX. These are usually based on either Berkeley or AT&T UNIX. For example,

Version	Company	Based on
AIX	IBM	AT & T and BSD
A/UX	Apple Computer	AT&T System V
HP-UX	Hewlett-Packard	BSD 4.3
SunOS	Sun Microsystems	BSD 4.3
ULTRIX	Digital Equipment Corp.	BSD 4.2
XENIX	Microsoft	AT&T Version 7

Keep in mind that these UNIX versions are very similar; if you learn to use one, you should have little trouble with any of the others.

Major Components of UNIX

The UNIX operating system consists of four main parts:

- *Kernel.* The *kernel* is the master control program of the computer. It resides in the computer's main memory, and it manages the computer's resources. It is the kernel that handles the switching necessary to provide multitasking.

- *Shell.* The part of UNIX that interprets user commands and passes them on to the kernel is called the *shell*.

- *File System.* UNIX organizes information into collections called *files*. You can put just about any kind of information into a file—a program you have written, a memo, data waiting to be analyzed, the manuscript for your next novel, even a letter to your mother. Files may be grouped together into collections called *directory files*, usually called *directories*.

- *Utilities.* A *utility* is a useful software tool that is included as a standard part of the UNIX operating system. Utilities are often called *commands*. UNIX provides a rich set of utilities for word processing, programming, database management, communications, etc.

UNIX Shells

Three different shells are commonly used today. The Bourne Shell was developed at AT&T by Steve Bourne; it is standard on AT&T System V UNIX. The C Shell was written by Bill Joy for Berkeley UNIX. The Korn Shell was written by David Korn at AT&T; it is based on the Bourne Shell, but it includes many of the features of the C Shell. Most UNIX installations offer all three of these shells; some have other shells as well. This book examines the Bourne, Korn, and C Shells.

Your Terminal

You will communicate with the computer using a *terminal*, which consists of a typewriter-like keyboard attached to a video display device. (You may still occasionally run across an old teletype terminal, which prints on a roll of paper instead of a video display.)

UNIX operates in what is called *full-duplex* mode. This means that any characters that you type on your terminal keyboard are first sent to the computer, which then echoes them back to your terminal to be displayed on the screen. For this to work correctly, you must tell the system what kind of terminal you are using. Many different terminals are available on the market; each type is identified by a code, called a *termcap* or *terminfo* code. These codes are typically abbreviations for the terminal model designation. For example,

Manufacturer	Model	Code
Applied Digital Data Systems	Regent 20	reg20
Digital Equipment Corp.	VT100	vt100

Hewlett-Packard	2621	hp2621
Lear-Siegler	ADM 3	adm3
Liberty Electronics	Freedom 100	f100
Perkin-Elmer	550	pe550
Sanyo	55	sanyo55
Televideo	925	tvi925
Tektronix	4015	tek4015
Wyse Technology	50	wyse50
Zenith Data Systems	19	z19

Your Printer

You'll want a way to print your files. (Paper output from a printer is usually called *hardcopy*.) A large computer installation may have a variety of printers. Individual printers are identified by a code, which usually indicates the type and location of the printer. To give you an idea of what these codes may look like, here are some of the hardcopy output devices available at Purdue University:

Location	Type	Code
Computing Center	Versatec Plotter	puccvp
Math Building	C. Itoh	mathci
Matthews Hall	Dataprinter	mthw
Owens Hall	Apple Laser Writer	owenlw

Your UNIX Account

Most UNIX systems require that you set up an account before you can use the computer; see your instructor, consultant, or system administrator about this. When your account is created, you should receive the following information:

- the name of the computer you'll be using

- an account or user name

- a password

Your account name is often called your *login*, because you use it to identify yourself when you "log in" to use the computer. (*Logging in* is the process of gaining access to the computer.) Your login will typically be some variation of your real name. It may consist of as many as eight letters or numbers; however, it must begin with a letter.

Your *password* tells the computer that you are who you say you are—passwords are meant to prevent unauthorized use of the computer. *Never share your password with anyone*. It is a good idea to change your password frequently—you will see how in the next chapter.

While you are setting up your account, it is a good idea to ask a few questions:

- Which variety of UNIX will I be using—AT&T or Berkeley?

- Which UNIX shell will I be using?

- What kind of terminal will I be using? What is its code name?

- Which printer will I use? What is its code name?

- What is the login procedure? (May I have that in writing please?)

Exercises

(1)   Define: (a) hardware; (b) software; (c) CPU; (d) main memory; (e) internal memory; (f) mass storage; (g) I/O device; (h) network; (i) terminal; (j) peripheral; (k) operating system; (l) multiuser; (m) multitasking; (n) kernel; (o) shell; (p) file; (q) directory file; (r) directory; (s) utility; (t) login; (u) password; (v) host; (w) server.

(2)   Large computer installations typically have several public terminal rooms. How many terminal rooms does your installation have? Where are they located?

(3)   Name the two most popular versions of UNIX. Which one runs on your machine?

(4)   Name the three most common UNIX shells. Which shell will you be using?

(5)   Who can you ask for help if you run into problems with your UNIX system?

(6)   How can you print your files? Where is the printer located? What is the code for the printer you will use?

(7)   What kind of terminal will you be using? What is its code?

2. Tutorial: Getting Started

In this chapter you will learn how to gain access to the computer. Unfortunately, UNIX installations do differ, so it is a good idea to have someone standing by to help with the specifics, especially the first time.

If you haven't done so already, ask your instructor, system administrator, or consultant about setting up an account. You should already know the name of the computer you'll be using, your account or login ("log-in") name, and your password.

The Terminal

Your next destination is the computer terminal room. Find a terminal and get comfortable. The terminal should have a keyboard, similar in many ways to the keyboard of a typewriter (Figure 2.1). However, the terminal keyboard has some important keys that are not found on a typewriter. See if you can locate the following five keys on your terminal:

(1) RETURN—Also called NEWLINE or ENTER key, the RETURN key is almost always located on the right hand side of the keyboard.

(2) CONTROL—This is usually on the left hand side of the keyboard. It is generally used in combination with another key, both keys being pressed simultaneously.

(3) ESCAPE—The usual position for this key is near the upper left corner of the keyboard.

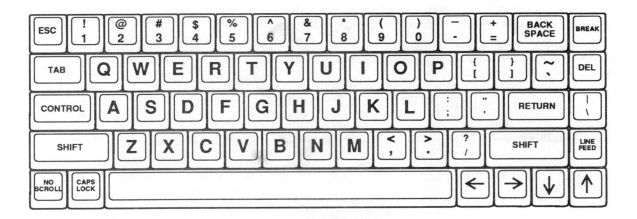

Figure 2.1. A typical computer keyboard. Note the locations of the ESCAPE (ESC), BREAK, and CONTROL (CTRL) keys. Also note that the keyboard depicted here has both a BACKSPACE key and a DELETE (DEL) key; one of these will usually serve as the erase key. Your computer keyboard may differ somewhat in the names and locations of the keys.

(4)   ERASE—This may appear as the BACKSPACE, DELETE, or RUBOUT key. Some keyboards do not have a separate erase key but instead use a combination of keys such as CONTROL+h. (Hold down CONTROL, and press the *h* key.)

(5)   BREAK—On some terminals this key is labeled RESET. It is used to alert the computer that you want to use it.

Now find the "on" switch. This may be hidden under the front edge of the keyboard or on the back panel of the terminal. (See if you can find the power cord—the switch may be close to the point where the cord enters the terminal.) Turn on the terminal, and allow it to warm up.

After a while, you should see a small, blinking line or rectangle on the terminal screen. This is the *cursor*. It shows where the next typed character will appear.

Connecting to the Computer

Now you must get the computer's attention. This is usually very easy if your terminal is directly wired to just one computer. Simply press the RETURN key:

```
RET
```

Some systems require that you alert the computer first by pressing RESET, BREAK, or CONTROL+BREAK. (For the latter command, press the BREAK key while holding down the CONTROL key.)

Things are a bit more complicated if you are using a modem to communicate with the computer over a telephone line. This requires that you have the computer's telephone number and that you know how to use your modem. The telephone number you can get from your instructor or system administrator; instructions on the use of the modem should have been included with the modem itself.

If several computers are tied into your system, you will be asked to specify the one you want. You may be asked

```
Which computer?
```

Or perhaps something like

```
Dial:
```

This is where you need to know the name of the computer on which you have an account. Just type in the computer name you were given, and press the RETURN key.

Logging In

You will know when you have reached your computer because it will identify itself and ask you to log in:

```
login:
```

Type in the login name you were given, then press the RETURN key. The computer will respond

```
password:
```

Now type in the password you were given, followed by RETURN. Note that YOUR PASSWORD DOES NOT APPEAR ON THE SCREEN. The idea is to prevent others from looking over your shoulder and learning your password. (You will see how to change the password later.)

If you make an error typing either your login name or password, the computer will tell you that your login is incorrect, and it will give you the chance to log in again:

```
Login incorrect
login:
```

You must then type in your login name, followed by your password.

Once you gain access to the machine, it may print a variety of messages, including

- Message of the day from the system administrator;

- Mail alert, telling you there is electronic mail waiting for you;

- Request that you set your terminal type.

Some UNIX systems ask about the terminal type each time you log in. The computer will give you an instruction such as

```
Set terminal type (adm3):
```

Or perhaps

```
TERM (adm3):
```

The text in parentheses is the *default terminal type*; unless you tell it otherwise, the computer will assume that this is the terminal you are using. If it is, then simply hit RETURN and continue on. If it is not, type in the code name for the type of terminal you are using. (This is something you should have obtained from your instructor or system administrator.) Then press RETURN.

UNIX Shell Prompt

At this point, you should see a *prompt,* which is simply the computer's way of telling you that it is ready to receive your instructions. If you are using the C Shell, the prompt might be a percent sign:

```
%
```

If you are using the Bourne Shell or the Korn Shell, the usual prompt is a dollar sign:

```
$
```

Other symbols are occasionally used for prompts, including the pound sign (#), the "greater than" sign (>), the asterisk (*), the "at" symbol (@), and the colon (:). In this book, we will use the following as our "generic" prompt, to take the place of either the percent sign or the dollar sign:

$

Setting the Terminal Type

If your UNIX system did not ask for your terminal type when you logged in, you will have to set the type yourself. The way you do this depends on which shell you are using. The **setenv** ("set environment") command is used with the C Shell. For example, to set up for a Digital Equipment Corporation VT100 terminal, you would type *

```
%setenv TERM vt100 RET
```

Alternatively, the **set term** ("set terminal") command may be used:

```
%set term = vt100 RET
```

Note that *term* is in lowercase letters and that an equals sign (=) is used.

If you are using the Bourne Shell or the Korn Shell, two commands are required to set the terminal type. First, set TERM equal to the terminal type:

```
$TERM=vt100 RET
```

Note that *TERM* is entirely in uppercase letters and that there are no spaces around the equals sign. Next, "export" TERM to make the information available to any utilities that need it:

```
$export TERM RET
```

Changing Your Password

It is a good idea to change your password frequently, to prevent unauthorized use of your account. The first thing to do is to think of a new password. A good password should be easy for you to remember, but difficult for someone else to figure out. Here are some good general rules for selecting a password:

- Choose a password that is at least six characters long.

- Combine numbers, uppercase letters, and lowercase letters.

- Make it memorable, but avoid common names and words.

---

* In the examples that follow, DO NOT TYPE IN THE PROMPT SYMBOL. You should enter only the characters that follow the prompt. Also, RET indicates that you should press the RETURN or NEWLINE key.

- Do not use your Social Security number, your telephone number, your login, or any variation of your login.

- Make sure the new password differs significantly from the old one.

Your particular computer installation may have other rules as well—consult your instructor or system administrator.

Once you have selected a password, type the command

$passwd RET

The system will ask you to type in your old password, which you should do, remembering to finish with a RETURN. Note that the password is not shown on the screen:

    Old password:

The computer will ask you to type in your new password. As before, the password does not appear on the screen:

    New password:

To ensure that there is no mistake, the computer will ask you to repeat your new password. This has to be done exactly as before, or the system will not accept the new password, and you will have to start over:

    Retype new password:
    $

You will know that the new password has been accepted when the prompt symbol appears. DO NOT GIVE YOUR PASSWORD TO ANYONE!

Some UNIX Commands

Now that you have set up your terminal, try a few UNIX commands to see how they work. Start with the **date** command. Simply type *date* after the prompt, and press the RETURN key:

$date RET

The computer will respond with the date and time. For example, if you were to give this command on Friday, August 13, 1999, at 8:35 pm (Eastern Standard Time), the response would be something like

    Fri Aug 13 20:35:41 EST 1999

Note that the time is given on the 24-hour clock.

Next try the **who** command. Type *who*, followed by RETURN:

$who RET

The computer will respond with a list of the users who are currently logged into the system. For example,

```
root        console    Aug 13    08:11
aadams      tty16      Aug 13    07:01
pgw         tty03      Aug 13    18:15
ben         tty18      Aug 13    11:32
jeff        tty12      Aug 13    09:45
```

The user's login name is listed first, followed by a code that identifies the line or "port" to which the user is connected.* The date and time that the user logged in are also shown.

Reading Your Mail

When you log in, the system checks to see if you have any unread electronic mail. If so, it will alert you with a message:

```
You have mail.
```

The message will vary somewhat from system to system; in some versions, for example, you will be told how many mail messages you have received. If you are using AT&T UNIX, you can read your mail by typing

$mailx RET

If you are using Berkeley UNIX, type

$mail RET

The system will respond with a list of the messages. For example,

```
U  1 wards   Thu Aug 12 15:27  554/26358  "Class Roster"
N  2 aadams  Fri Aug 13 8:59  40/1527  "Lunch"
N  3 gwc     Fri Aug 13  9:47  15/440  "Research Notes"
&
```

A *U* in the first column indicates an unread message left over from the last time you logged in; an *N* indicates a new message. The messages are numbered (from 1 to 3 in this case). The login name of the sender is shown, along with the date and time the message was received and the number of lines and characters the message contains (lines/characters). Finally, the subject of the message is given in quotes.

The ampersand (&) on the last line is the *mail prompt*. If you wish to read one of the messages, simply type in its number after the prompt and press RETURN:

&2 RET

---

* Here, "tty" stands for "teletype." When UNIX was first developed, teletype machines were commonly used as terminals. That is no longer true, but "tty" is still used to mean terminal.

This will cause the second message to appear:

```
Message 2:
From aadams Fri Aug 13 8:59:01 1999
Date: Fri Aug 13 8:59:01
From: aadams (Abigail Adams)
To: (Your login name)
Subject: Lunch
Let's get together for lunch at 12:45 today. Okay?
&
```

Once you have finished, you can leave the mail utility by typing *q* (for *quit*):

&q RET

Electronic mail—including the ways to send, save, and delete mail—is discussed in more detail in Part IV.

Reading the UNIX Manual

Many UNIX systems come equipped with a detailed on-line manual that you can read using the **man** command. The manual describes the commands that are available on the system. To see how this is done, try the following command:

$man cal RET

The **cal** command is one that we will use in later chapters; it displays a calendar on the screen. If your system has the on-line manual, you should see a description of **cal**. (For more information on how to make sense of the manual, see Appendix A.) Otherwise, you will see the message

```
man: Command not found.
```

Logging Out

When you are finished working on the computer, you must "log out." This tells the system that you are finished using it. DO NOT TURN OFF THE TERMINAL WITHOUT LOGGING OUT FIRST. On some UNIX systems, your account will remain open even if your terminal is turned off. This invites the unscrupulous to get into the system and make mischief.

If you are using the C Shell (% prompt), try this command to log out:

%logout RET

If you are using the Bourne or Korn Shell ($ prompt), try this command:

$exit RET

If this doesn't work, try holding down the CONTROL key while striking *d*:

$ CTRL + d

If none of these works, ask for help!

Summary

Each of the commands listed here is typed after the prompt symbol (usually % or $).

Setting the Terminal Type (C Shell)

```
setenv TERM type RET
set term = type RET
```
         set terminal to *type*
         (alternative to `setenv`)

Setting the Terminal Type (Bourne or Korn Shell)

```
TERM=type RET
export TERM RET
```
         set terminal to *type* (use with `export`)
         (First set TERM=*type*)

Changing Your Password

```
passwd RET
```
         change password

Miscellaneous UNIX Commands

```
date RET
who RET
man command RET
```
         give current date and time
         list users currently logged in
         show the manual page describing *command*

Logging Out

```
logout RET
exit RET
CTRL + d
```
         logout for C Shell
         logout for Bourne or Korn Shell
         optional logout command

Exercises

The exercises marked with an asterisk (*) are intended to be done at the keyboard.

(1)   Define (a) cursor; (b) default; (c) login name; (d) logging out; (e) prompt; (f) shell.

(2)   What kinds of terminals are connected to your UNIX system? Examine several different terminals and locate the RETURN, CONTROL, ESCAPE, ERASE, and BREAK keys, and the on/off switches.

(3)   Which of the following would be good passwords for someone named Glynda Jones Davis, whose login name, phone number, and Social Security number are "gjdavis," 555-2525, and 632-10-6854, respectively? Explain your reasons.

```
cat             7cattz          Jones           jones

Smith           sivadjg         NotSmith        532106854

5552525         Glynda          t555s632        kangaroo

KRoo2           tiPPecanoe      tylerTwo        x27woKzZ
```

(4)* See if your terminal has a NO SCROLL key. This key is supposed to "freeze" the terminal display. Press it and type your name. What happens on the screen? Now press NO SCROLL again. What do you see?

(5)* Does your keyboard have a CAPS LOCK or CASE key? If so, press it and type something on the keyboard. What does this key do?

(6)* UNIX is *case-sensitive*; it distinguishes between upper- and lower-case letters. Try the commands listed below and note what each one does (if anything):

```
WHO RET
who am i RET
WHO AM I RET
DATE RET
echo Hello RET
ECHO Hello RET
cal 1990 RET
CAL 1990 RET
```

Part II
THE UNIX FILE SYSTEM

3. The UNIX File System

A UNIX *file* is a collection of related information—anything from a chocolate cake recipe to a computer program. Ordinary UNIX files are organized into special files called *directories*. The distinction between an ordinary file and a directory file is simple: ordinary files hold information; directories hold ordinary files and other directories. In this chapter, you will learn how the UNIX system keeps track of your files and directories.

Home and Working Directories

When you first log into your UNIX account, you enter what is known as your *home directory*. This is where you will keep any files or directories that you create. The name of your home directory is the same as your login name.

After you have logged into your home directory, you are free to move to other directories in the system. Whichever directory you happen to be working in at the time is called your *current* or *working directory*. When you first log in, your working directory is your home directory.

Each user on the system is given a home directory. On a typical large UNIX system, there may be hundreds of these home directories, each containing scores of other files and directories.

The UNIX File Tree

Figure 3.1 is a simplified diagram of a typical UNIX system. It looks something like an upside-down tree, with its root at the top. In fact, the directory at the very top, the one that contains all of the other directories, is called the **root**. Various other directories reside inside the **root** directory:

bin This directory contains the software for the shell and the most commonly used UNIX commands. Although **bin** is short for "binary," you may want to think of it as a "bin" holding many useful software tools.

dev The name is short for "devices"; this directory holds the software needed to operate peripheral devices such as terminals and printers.

usr Users' home directories are kept here. On some large systems there may be several directories holding user files.

etc Various administrative files are kept in this directory, including the list of users that are authorized to use the system, as well as their passwords.

tmp This directory holds temporary files.

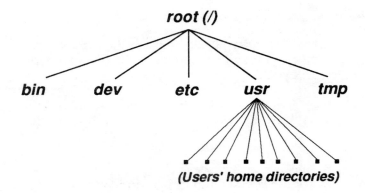

Figure 3.1. Directory structure of a typical UNIX system. Users' home directories are kept in the directory *usr* in this system.

Your particular UNIX system may be set up a bit differently, but all UNIX systems have a *root* directory at the top.

A directory will sometimes be referred to as the "parent" or the "child" of another directory. For example, *root* is the parent of *bin, dev, usr, etc,* and *tmp*; these directories, in turn, are the children of *root*. (Child directories are often called *subdirectories*.) Note that every directory except *root* has exactly one parent, but may have many children.

File and Directory Names

Every file and directory has a name. The name of your home directory is the same as your login, and you normally cannot rename it. However, you must choose names for any other files and directories you make. UNIX file names may comprise from one to fourteen of the following characters, in any combination:

- Uppercase letters (A to Z)

- Lowercase letters (a to z)

- Numerals (0 to 9)

- Period (.), underscore (_), comma (,)

The file name should not contain spaces, or any of the following special characters:

        & * \ | [ ] { } $ < > ( ) # ? ' " / ; ^ !

It is a good idea to choose reasonably short names (to save typing) that convey information about the contents of the file. Also, avoid file names that *begin* with a period (.), at least for the present.

This book follows the convention that ordinary file names are given in lowercase letters, while directory names (except for users' home directories) are capitalized. This will help you distinguish at a glance directories from ordinary files.

Absolute Pathnames

To use a file in your current directory, all you need is the file's name. However, if the file is located in another directory, you will need to know the file's *pathname*. A pathname is an address that shows the file's position in the file system.

Absolute or *full pathnames* give the location of a file in relation to the top of the file system. The simplest full pathname is for the *root* directory, which is represented by a slash:

/

The absolute pathnames for the *root*'s child directories, shown in Figure 3.1, are

/bin   */dev*   */etc*   */usr*   */tmp*

Note that each of these begins with a slash (/), which tells you that the path starts at the *root*. All absolute pathnames are preceded by a slash.

Figure 3.2 shows *usr* and two of the home directories it contains (*jack* and *jill*). You have already seen that the pathname for *usr* is

/usr

The full pathname for the user directory *jill* is

/usr/jill

This is called the pathname of *jill* because it tells what path to follow to get from the *root* directory to *jill*. In this case, the path goes from the *root* directory, to the directory *usr*, and finally to *jill*. Continuing further, the subdirectory *Marsupials* has the absolute pathname

/usr/jill/Marsupials

Ordinary files also have absolute pathnames. For example, the pathname of the file *wombat* is

/usr/jill/Marsupials/wombat

This means that *wombat* may be found by starting at the *root*, moving down to the directory *usr,* then to the user directory *jill*, to the directory *Marsupials*, and finally to the file *wombat* itself.

You may have noticed that the slash (/) serves two purposes in writing these pathnames. The first slash in the sequence stands for the *root*; the other slashes serve merely as separators between the file names.

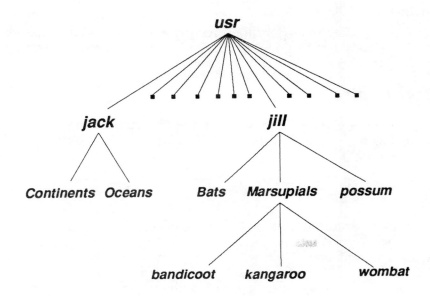

Figure 3.2. The *usr* directory, showing the two home directories *jack* and *jill*. A large UNIX system may contain hundreds of home directories.

Relative Pathnames

As you can easily imagine by now, full pathnames can become long and unwieldy. More often than not, you are interested in the position of a file or directory relative to your working directory. *Relative pathnames* start from working directory rather than the *root*.

When writing out a relative pathname, a single period or dot (.) is the shorthand notation for your current working directory. Similarly, two dots (..) are used to signify the *parent* of your working directory—the one above it in the directory structure. These are usually called *dot* and *dotdot*. Hence

> . ("*dot*") → current working directory

> .. ("*dotdot*") → parent of the working directory

For files in the current directory, the relative pathname is easy: it is simply the name of the file. Suppose you were working in the directory *jack* shown in Figure 3.2. The relative pathnames of the two directories in *jack* would be

> *Continents*   *Oceans*

The parent of *jack* is *usr*. Therefore, the relative pathname of *usr* would be

> . .

Suppose now that you wanted the relative pathname of the directory that contains *usr*, which is the *root* directory. From the directory *jack* this would be

../..

To find the **Marsupials** directory from the directory **jack**, you would first move up to **usr** (represented by **dotdot**), then down to **jill**, and finally down to **Marsupials** itself. Putting this altogether, the relative pathname becomes

> *../jill/Marsupials*

While absolute pathnames always begin with a slash (/), representing the root directory, relative pathnames begin either with **dotdot** (..), or the name of a file or directory in your current working directory.

Listing Files

You now know how to write absolute pathnames and relative pathnames, but you may reasonably wonder what good this is. To answer that, consider how pathnames may be used with a few UNIX commands. Start with the **ls** ("list") command.

Suppose **jack** is working in his home directory, and he wants to remind himself which files he has in his home directory. He would type the command

    $ ls RET

The response would be

    Continents Oceans

Now suppose **jack** wants to know what **jill** has in her **Marsupials** directory. From his home directory, he would use the **ls** command with the pathname of **Marsupials**:

    $ ls ../jill/Marsupials RET

The computer's answer would be

    bandicoot kangaroo wombat

Thus, without leaving home, **jack** can list files in a distant directory—even a directory belonging to another user—if he knows the directory's pathname.*

Hidden Files and Directories

A *hidden* (or *invisible*) file is one that is not listed when you use the simple **ls** command. A file or directory will be hidden if its name begins with a period. For example,

> *.hidden   .jim   .a3_cr5   .lost   .profile   .login   .   ..*

---

* Of course, **jack** would never examine or use **jill**'s files without her express permission. Most computer users respect the rights of others to keep their UNIX files private. Those who violate these rights may find themselves thrown off the system. If she wishes, **jill** can also restrict access to her files—see Appendix B for details on how this is done.

would all be hidden—they would not be listed by the simple **ls** command. To list all of the files in a directory, including the hidden ones, requires the **ls –a** ("list all") command. Suppose, for example, that *jack* is working in his home directory, and he types

     $ls –a⎡RET⎤

He would see

       .   ..   Continents Oceans

Similarly, if *jack* were to use this command with the pathname of *jill*'s **Marsupials** directory, he would see something like this:

     $ls –a ../jill/Marsupials⎡RET⎤
     .   ..   bandicoot   kangaroo   wombat

Note that *dot* (.) and *dotdot* (..) are both names of hidden directories, and that both appear when *jack* uses the **ls –a** command. Remember, *dot* is just another name for the current directory, while *dotdot* refers to the parent of the current directory. These two hidden entries always appear whenever the **ls –a** command is used.

Renaming and Moving Files

The **ls** command takes one pathname; now consider a command that uses two. The **mv** ("move") command has the general form

    mv *pathname1 pathname2*

This can be interpreted to mean "move the file found at *pathname1* to the position specified by *pathname2*." To see how this works, consider how *jill* might tidy up her home directory using **mv**.

The file name *possum* is wrong because the proper name for the animal is "opossum." If *jill* is still working in her home directory, the pathname of the file *possum* is just the file name. To change the name of the file without changing its location, she simply uses **mv** with the new name:

     $mv possum opossum⎡RET⎤

This tells UNIX "move the contents of *possum* (in the current directory) into the file *opossum* (also in the current directory)." Since there is no existing *opossum* file, one is created, and the old file name disappears.

Next *jill* remembers that the opossum is a marsupial, and therefore should be moved to the **Marsupials** directory. The **mv** command will do the trick:

     $mv opossum Marsupials⎡RET⎤

This means "move *opossum* from the current directory into the **Marsupials** directory." Thus *jill* can use the **mv** command twice, once to rename a file, and again to move it to another directory. The end result is shown in Figure 3.3.

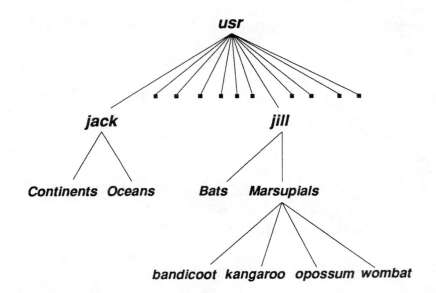

Figure 3.3. The *usr* directory after changing the file name from *possum* to *opossum*, and then moving the file to the *Marsupials* directory.

jill could have moved the file and renamed it at the same time using the command

```
$mv possum Marsupials/opossum RET
```

This means "move the contents of *possum* to the *Marsupials* directory and into a file named *opossum*."

Creating a File

There are four common ways to create a UNIX file:

(1) Copy an existing file.

(2) Redirect the "standard output" from a UNIX utility.

(3) Open a new file using a text editor.

(4) Write a computer program that opens new files.

Of these, (1) and (2) are considered in this chapter; the others are covered later in the book.

Copying Files

The **cp** ("copy") command has the general form

> **cp** *pathname1 pathname2*

This means "copy the file found at *pathname1* and place the copy in the position specified by *pathname2*." Suppose that *jack* has developed a sudden interest in wombats and asks *jill* for a copy of her file on the subject. From her home directory, *jill* uses the command

```
$cp Marsupials/wombat ../jack/Continents RET
```

to make a copy of the *wombat* file and put it in the *Continents* directory. The result is shown in Figure 3.4.

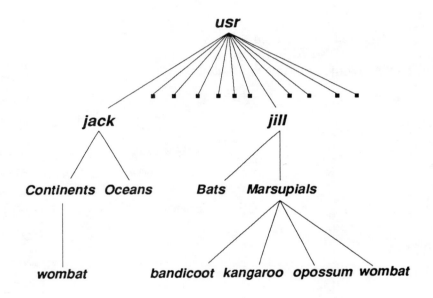

Figure 3.4. The *usr* directory after *jill* places a copy of *wombat* in the directory *Continents*.

Creating a File by Redirection

The second method of creating a new file is to redirect the output of a command. In other words, instead of displaying the results of the command on the screen, UNIX puts the results into a file. As an example, consider what happens if *jill* moves to her *Marsupials* directory and issues the **ls** command:

```
$ls RET
bandicoot kangaroo  oppossum  wombat
```

Suppose now that she wants to redirect this list into a file named *filelist*. She does this using the redirection symbol (>):

```
$ls > filelist RET
$
```

This time, nothing appears on the screen because the output was rerouted into the file. In UNIX jargon, the information was *redirected* from the *standard output* (i.e., the terminal screen) to the file. If *jill* lists her files now, she will see that there is a new one:

```
$ls RET
bandicoot filelist kangaroo oppossum wombat
```

Redirection is powerful and convenient, but it can be dangerous. If you redirect the output into a file that already exists, the original contents of the file will be lost.

Exercises

None of these exercises requires the computer.

(1)   Which of the following would be valid names for ordinary UNIX files? Explain.

foo	guess?	book.chap1	BOOK.chap2
2good2Btrue	{2bad}	>right>	<left<
name	rank*	serial#	^up^
el_paso	w.lafayette	New York City	/slash\

(2)   Which of the following would be valid directory names? Why or why not?

doo_wa	dir1	Dir2	Directory.3
*Hook	|Line|	"Sinker"	Money.$
Game	Set	Match	Sticks
[Groucho]	'Chico'	Harpo.#	Karl?

Exercises 3–8 refer to the hypothetical UNIX file system shown in Figure 3.4.

(3)   What are the absolute pathnames for *root*, *bin*, *jill*, and *kangaroo*?

(4)   Suppose that *Marsupials* is now your working directory. What are the relative pathnames of *root*, *bin*, *jill*, and *kangaroo*?

(5)   *jack* has two subdirectories, *Continents* and *Oceans.* (a) What are the absolute pathnames of *Continents* and *Oceans*? (b) From *Oceans*, what are the relative pathnames of the *root, etc*, and *bandicoot*? (Hint: it may be helpful in this and following problems to sketch the directory structure as you go along.)

(6)   Imagine that *jack* sets up additional subdirectories to hold geographical information. *Continents* contains *Africa*, *Antarctica*, *Asia*, *Australia*, *Europe*, *NAmerica*, and *SAmerica*. Each of these directories contains subdirectories for individual countries or regions. For example, *NAmerica* contains the subdirectories

Canada, *CentralAm*, *Mexico*, and *USA*. Assuming every file and directory to be in its proper place, give the absolute pathnames of the directories (a) *Norway*; (b) *India*; (c) *Egypt*; (d) *Argentina*.

(7)   Suppose *jack*'s working directory is *USA*. Show the commands he would use to (a) list the contents of the *Marsupials* directory belonging to *jill*; (b) list the contents of *Australia*; (c) make a copy of *jill*'s file *kangaroo*, and place it under the name *kangaroo* in his *Australia* directory.

(8)   The directory *Canada* has twelve subdirectories, one for each of the ten provinces and two territories. Suppose *jack*'s working directory is *SAmerica*. Show the commands he would use to (a) list the contents of *BC*, the directory for British Columbia, Canada; (b) place a copy of the file for Vancouver, British Columbia, in the directory *jill*.

(9)   If the standard output is the terminal screen, what is the standard input?

4. Tutorial: Working with Files

In this chapter, you will learn how to create calendar files using the UNIX **cal** utility. Then you will see how to use various commands to manipulate these files. All of your work will take place in your home directory—you'll see how to make subdirectories in the next chapter.

Displaying a Calendar

The UNIX utility **cal** will display a calendar for any month of any year from 1 to 9999. To see how this works, first log in and set your terminal. Then type the command

```
$cal 5 1999 RET
```

This tells **cal** to produce a calendar for the fifth month of 1999. The response is

```
    May 1999
 S  M Tu  W Th  F  S
                   1
 2  3  4  5  6  7  8
 9 10 11 12 13 14 15
16 17 18 19 20 21 22
23 24 25 26 27 28 29
30 31
```

The **cal** utility also allows you to display the calendar for an entire year. Type

```
$cal 1999 RET
```

A calendar for the year 1999 should have appeared on your screen, although it probably scrolled by too fast for you to read it all. Don't worry; in a moment you will see how to save this calendar in a file.

Redirection

Before you can create a new file, you must select a proper name for it. (You might want to review the rules for naming a UNIX file given in the previous chapter.) Remember to use relatively short, descriptive file names. A good name for a file holding the 1999 calendar might be *1999.* Type

```
$cal 1999 > 1999 RET
```

This time, the calendar does not appear on the screen; instead, the standard output from **cal** has been redirected into the file *1999.* The arrow (>) is the *redirection symbol.*

Warning: Since there was no file named *1999* in your home directory, the redirection operation created one. However, if you already had a file named *1999*, the new information would have been written over anything previously in the file.

Listing Your Files

How do you know that a new file has been created? You can use the **ls** command to show the names of the files in your working directory. The name of the new file should appear:

```
$ls RET
1999
```

Viewing a File with cat

Suppose you want to see the *contents* of a file, not just its name. One way to do this is by the use of the **cat** ("concatenate") command. To look at the *1999* file, type

```
$cat 1999 RET
```

This displays the file, but it scrolls by so fast that the first few lines cannot be read. Fortunately, UNIX provides a more convenient means of viewing files.

Viewing with more (BSD UNIX)

To display a file, one screen at a time, Berkeley UNIX provides the **more** command:

```
$more 1999 RET
```

This will display as much of the file as will fit on the screen at one time. If the entire file does not fit, a message will appear in the lower corner of the screen, something like

```
--More--
```

This indicates that more of the file remains to be seen. To see more, simply press the space bar (SPACE). To exit the file without viewing the whole thing, type *q* (for *quit*). No RETURN is needed:

```
q
```

Viewing with pg (AT&T System V UNIX)

To display a file, one screenful at a time, AT&T UNIX offers the **pg** ("page") command:

```
$pg 1999 RET
```

This shows as much of the file *1999* as will fit on the screen at one time. A colon (:) appears at the bottom of the screen to indicate that more of the file remains to be seen. To see the next screenful, press RETURN; to quit, type *q* or *Q*:

```
q
```

Printing a File

If you are using Berkeley UNIX, you can print the contents of a file with the **lpr** ("line printer") command. The simplest form of this command is

```
$lpr 1999 RET
```

On AT&T UNIX, use the **lp** command:

```
$lp 1999 RET
```

If your computer system has more than one printer attached to it, the simple line printer command will send your files to the *default printer*. You can specify another printer with the the **–P** or **–d** option. To do this, you first have to know the code for the printer you are to use; ask your instructor, consultant, or system administrator. On Berkeley UNIX you would type the following command, making sure to insert the proper printer code in place of *code*:

```
$lpr -Pcode 1999 RET
```

Note that there is a space before –P and before the file name, but not between the –P and the printer code. On AT&T UNIX, you would type the following command, inserting the printer code in place of *code*:

```
$lp -dcode 1999 RET
```

Here again, there is a space before –d and before the file name, but not between the –d and the printer code.

Chaining Files Together

Your next task is to make a calendar for the summer months of 1999. First use **cal** to make a calendar for June 1999, and redirect it into a file named *june99*:

```
$cal 6 1999 > june99 RET
```

Next make a calendar file for July 1999:

```
$cal 7 1999 > july99 RET
```

Now use the **cat** command on the two files *june99* and *july99*:

```
$cat june99 july99 RET
```

The **cat** command is the same one you used before to view the contents of the file. When given a single file name, **cat** simply displays the contents of that file; when two or more filenames are used together, **cat** displays all of the files, one after another. Use **cat** again, only this time redirect the output into a file named *summer99*:

```
$cat june99 july99 > summer99 RET
```

This creates a new file containing a two-month calendar. List the files:

```
$ls RET
1999  july99  june99  summer99
```

Appending to a File

You are not yet finished with your *summer99* file; you need to add the month of August. UNIX allows you to add information to the end of an existing file. To append the calendar for August 1999 to the file *summer99*, type the following line, making sure to use the *append symbol* (>>):

```
$cal 8 1999 >> summer99 RET
```

Had you used the regular redirection symbol (>), the calendar for August would have replaced the calendars for June and July that were already in the file. Instead, August was added to the end of the summer file.

Copying and Renaming a File

Now try out the **cp** command. Make a copy of the file *summer99*, and call the copy *SUMM99*. Type

```
$cp summer99 SUMM99 RET
```

This means "copy the contents of the file *summer99* into the file *SUMM99*." In this case, there is no existing file with the name *SUMM99*, so one is created. Use **ls** to check that the new file appears:

```
$ls RET
1999  SUMM99  july99  june99  summer99
```

There is just one small problem: the convention in this book is to use lowercase letters for file names, and to capitalize directory names. (You don't have to do this, but it helps distinguish files from directories.) *SUMM99* is an ordinary file, not a directory, so you should give it a different name. A good descriptive name might be *vacation99*. Use the **mv** command to change the file name:

```
$mv SUMM99 vacation99 RET
```

If you issue a **list** command now, you will see the new file name *vacation99*, but not the old name *SUMM99*:

```
$ls RET
1999  july99  june99  summer99  vacation99
```

The difference between **cp** (copy) and **mv** (move) is that **cp** creates a new file, leaving the old file intact, while **mv** simply renames the old file.

Removing Unneeded Files

When a file is no longer useful, you should remove it so that it won't take up valuable storage space. This is done with the **rm** command, which takes the pathname of the file to be removed. Since you probably don't need two copies of the summer 1999 calendar, remove one of them. Type

```
$rm vacation99 RET
```

Use the **ls** command to check that the file is really gone:

```
$ls RET
1999   july99   june99   summer99
```

Summary

Each command is typed in after the UNIX shell prompt, and each is terminated by a RETURN. Note that *file, file1,* and *file2* may be simple file names, or pathnames.

Making Calendars

cal *m year*	show a calendar for the *m*th month of *year*
cal *year*	show a calendar for *year*
cal *year* > *file*	redirect calendar for *year* into *file*
cal *year* >> *file*	append calendar for *year* to *file*

Listing and Viewing Files

ls	list files in working directory
cat *file*	show contents of *file* all at once.
more *file*	show contents of *file* one screen at a time. Press SPACE to continue or *q* to quit. (BSD UNIX)
pg *file*	Like **more**. Press RETURN to see the next screen, *q* to quit. (AT&T UNIX)

Printing Files

lpr *file*	send *file* to default line printer (BSD UNIX)
lp *file*	send *file* to default line printer (AT&T UNIX)
lpr -P*code file*	send *file* to printer designated by *code* (BSD)
lpr -d*code file*	send *file* to printer designated by *code* (AT&T)

Copying, Renaming, and Removing Files

cp *file1 file2*	copy *file1* into *file2*; retain both copies of the file.
mv *file1 file2*	move (i.e., rename) *file1* to *file2*; retain only *file2*.
rm *file*	remove (i.e., delete) *file*

Exercises

The exercises marked with an asterisk (*) are to be done at the keyboard.

(1)   What are the rules for selecting UNIX file names?

(2)* Because of the need to make certain adjustments to the calendar, the month of September, 1752, was a very unusual one. What was different about it?

(3)* The **echo** command takes a line that you type in and repeats it back on the screen. Thus if you type

```
echo "This is fun!" RET
```

The computer will respond with

```
This is fun!
```

Redirect this phrase into a file named *fun*.

(4)* Using the commands **who**, **who am i**, and **date**, append to the *fun* file a list of the users currently logged onto the computer, your login, and the current date.

(5)* A hidden file has a name that begins with a period (.). Use the **cal** utility and the redirection operator (>) to create a file named *.hidden*, then use **ls** to list your files. Do you see the *.hidden* file? Now try the **ls −a** command. Does *.hidden* appear? What other hidden file entries do you see?

5. Tutorial: Working with Directories

Until now, all of your UNIX work has taken place within your home directory. If you have faithfully followed the examples in the text and worked through all of the end-of-chapter exercises, your file system should resemble Figure 5.1. You are now ready to create new subdirectories inside your home directory.

Figure 5.1. Your file system after completing the previous chapter. All of your files reside in your home directory; you have no subdirectories yet.

Making a Subdirectory

It's time to make a directory to hold the calendars you made in the previous chapter. The first step is to select an appropriate name for the new directory. The rules for naming directories are essentially the same as for files except that it's a good idea to capitalize directory names to distinguish them from ordinary files. A descriptive name for the new directory would be *Cal*. (Note that the directory name *Cal* differs from the **cal** command—remember, UNIX is case-sensitive.)

If you haven't already done so, log in and set up your terminal. Then type the **mkdir** ("make directory") command, followed by the new directory name. Remember to capitalize the directory name:

    $mkdir Cal RET

Now try the **ls** command to see that the new directory exists:

    $ls RET
    1999 Cal fun july99 june99 summer99

Cal should appear, along with the names of the files you made before. Your file system should resemble Figure 5.2.

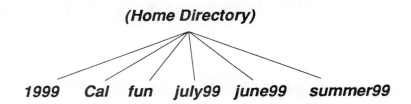

Figure 5.2. Your file system after creating the subdirectory *Cal*. At this point, *Cal* contains no files.

Moving Files between Directories

Your new subdirectory is empty. Put the file *1999* into the new directory using the **mv** ("move") command:

```
$mv 1999 Cal RET
```

This moves the file *1999* inside the directory *Cal* (see Figure 5.3). Recall that you used **mv** before to rename a file; this same command is used to move a file to a different directory.

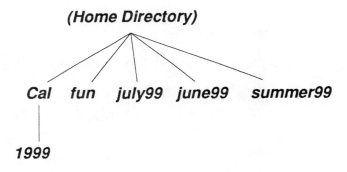

Figure 5.3. Your file system after moving the file *1999* into *Cal*.

Making Another Subdirectory

Your next task is to create yet another subdirectory inside *Cal* to hold monthly calendars. A good, descriptive name for this directory is *Months*. Since this is to go inside *Cal*, the relative pathname of the new directory will be *Cal/Months*. Type

```
$mkdir Cal/Months RET
```

Remember to capitalize *Months* to emphasize that it is a directory name. With the creation of *Months,* your directory structure should resemble the one in Figure 5.4.

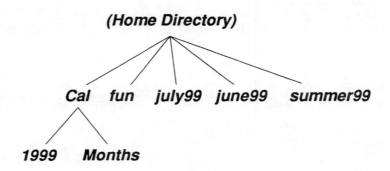

Figure 5.4. Making a directory inside *Cal*. Because the new directory will hold monthly calendars, it is called *Months*.

Now move the files *july99* and *june99* into *Months* using the **mv** command:

```
$mv july99 Cal/Months RET
$mv june99 Cal/Months RET
```

The **ls** command should show that these two files are no longer in the home directory:

```
$ls RET
Cal   fun   summer99
```

At this point, your directory structure should look something like Figure 5.5.

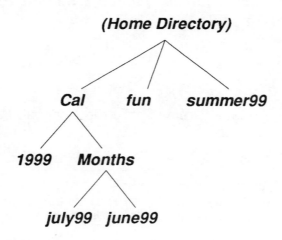

Figure 5.5. Directory structure after moving *july99* and *june99* into the subdirectory *Months*.

Working in a Distant Directory

The simple **ls** command only lists files in the current working directory. To list files in another directory, you must give **ls** that directory's pathname. Thus, to list the files in *Months* from your home directory, type

    $ls Cal/Months RET

You should see

    july99 june99

You can view the contents of the file *july99* from your home directory using the **cat** command with the appropriate pathname:

    $cat Cal/Months/july99 RET

To view the file one screen at a time use either the **more** or the **pg** command:

    $more Cal/Months/july99 RET

    or

    $pg Cal/Months/july99 RET

Changing Directories

You can change your current working directory using the **cd** ("change directory") command with the pathname of the target directory. Thus, to move to the subdirectory *Months*, you would type

    $cd Cal/Months RET

Now your working directory is *Months*. A simple **ls** will now show the files in *Months*:

    $ls RET
    july99 june99

To return to your home directory, you *could* use **cd** with either the absolute or the relative pathname of your home directory. However, there is a much easier way. Simply use **cd** without giving a pathname at all:

    $cd RET

This will always get you back to your home directory, regardless of where you are in the file structure. The **ls** command now should list the files and directories contained in your home directory:

```
$ ls RET
Cal   fun   summer99
```

Finding Yourself

As you might imagine, it is easy to get lost among the hundreds of directories in a large UNIX system. The **pwd** ("print working directory") command always displays the absolute pathname of your current working directory:

```
$ pwd RET
```

Removing Directories

A directory that is no longer needed may be removed by means of the **rmdir** ("remove directory") command. From your home directory, try removing the subdirectory *Cal*. Type

```
$ rmdir Cal RET
```

The computer will respond with a message such as

```
rmdir: Cal: Directory not empty
```

You cannot remove a directory unless it is first emptied of files and other directories. This is a safety feature, intended to prevent you from accidentally throwing away files that you meant to keep.

Summary

Each of these commands is typed in after the UNIX prompt, and each is terminated by a RETURN. *Dir* and *file* represent the pathnames of a directory and a file, respectively.

```
mkdir Dir       make a directory with the pathname Dir
mv file Dir     move file into the directory Dir
cd Dir          change to directory Dir
cd              change to home directory
rmdir Dir       remove (i.e., delete) the directory Dir
```

Exercises

The exercises marked with an asterisk (*) are to be done at the keyboard.

(1)   What are the rules for naming UNIX directories?

(2)*   What is the absolute pathname of your home directory?

(3)*   Create a new directory *Misc* and move the file *fun* inside this new directory.

(4)* Without leaving your home directory, create a directory named **Vacations** inside **Cal**. Then move **summer99** into this new directory.

(5)   Prepare a sketch of your directory structure after completing Exercises 2–4.

Part III
THE VISUAL EDITOR

6. The vi Editor

A *text editor* is a program that you can use to create and modify UNIX files. UNIX systems typically offer a choice of text editors: **ed**, **ex**, and **vi** are the most common. In this chapter, you will learn about UNIX text editors in general, and about **vi** in particular.

How a Text Editor Works

Regardless of the text editor you choose, the process of editing a text file can be summarized like this:

(1) You start the editor and give it the name of a file to edit.

(2) If you specified an existing file, the editor makes a copy of it and places the copy in a temporary workspace called the *work buffer*. If you are creating a new file, the editor simply opens up an empty work buffer.

(3) You use editor commands to add, delete, and/or change the text in the work buffer. When you are satisfied with the changes you have made, you tell the editor to "write into the file."

(4) The editor saves the contents of the work buffer in the file. If you are editing an existing file, the editor replaces the original file with the updated version in the buffer.

Note that you do not work directly on the file, but only on the copy that is in the buffer. This means that if you leave the editor without writing your changes into the file, the changes are lost, and the original file is not altered.

Line and Screen Editors

All editors do much the same things, but some are decidedly easier to use than others. The original UNIX editor **ed** is called a *line editor*, because it makes changes in the buffer line by line. To make a change using a line editor, you must first specify the line where you want the change to be made, and then you must specify the change itself. This can be a lot of work for even minor changes. Furthermore, it can be difficult to keep in mind the way the changes fit into the text as a whole because you are working with just one line or group of lines at a time.

A *full screen editor*, on the other hand, allows you to view and to work with as much of the work buffer as will fit on your screen. You can easily move the cursor around the screen, making changes to characters, words, and paragraphs as well as lines. Any changes you make are always apparent because the screen is updated immediately. And you can see clearly how the changes affect the rest of the text because you can view many lines at the same time.

Screen editors are sometimes called *visual editors*; **vi** is short for "visual." The **vi** editor is a screen editor that was originally written for Berkeley UNIX, but is now found on almost all UNIX systems. It is the editor discussed in this book.

vi Modes

To use **vi,** you have to know something about its operating modes (see Figure 6.1). When you first enter the **vi** editor, it is set to the *command mode*. What this means is that **vi** will treat all keystrokes as editing commands, and not as text to be entered into the file. Pressing RETURN, BACKSPACE or the space bar while in the command mode moves the cursor without introducing new lines or spaces into the text.

To add text to the file, you must switch to the *insert mode*, which you can do using any of the following commands:

i   insert text to the left of the current cursor location

a   add text to the right of the cursor

R   Replace (type over) existing text

o   open a new line below the current line, and move the cursor there

O   Open a new line above the current line, and move the cursor there

None of these insert-mode commands appears on the screen, but everything typed in afterward does. Pressing the ESCAPE key returns **vi** to the command mode.

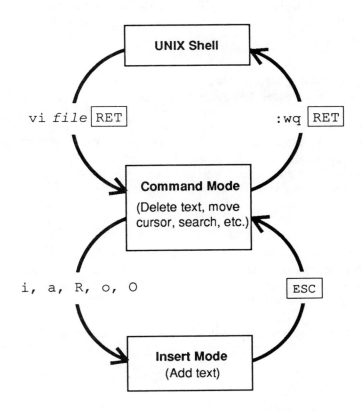

Figure 6.1. Operating modes of the visual editor **vi.**

In general, you use the insert mode when adding text to the file, and the command mode for everything else (moving around the file, deleting text, etc.).

Perhaps the most common difficulty that beginning **vi** users have is remembering which mode they are working in. When in doubt, hit the ESCAPE key a couple of times to get back to the command mode. (If the terminal beeps when you press ESCAPE, that is a signal that you are in the command mode.)

Buffers and More Buffers

Recall that **vi** actually works on a copy of the file in the work buffer. While using **vi**, you have access to other buffers as well. There are 36 of these:

- unnamed buffer

- named buffers "a, "b, "c, . . . ,"z

- numbered buffers "1, "2, "3, . . . ,"9

The *unnamed buffer* is sometimes called the *general-purpose buffer*. When you change or delete text, the old text is not thrown away immediately. Instead, **vi** moves the old material into the unnamed buffer, and holds it there until you change or delete more material. The advantage of this is that it allows you to change your mind and restore the deleted text using the "undo" command:

```
u
```

This puts the old text back where it came from. Since **vi** has only one unnamed buffer, the **undo** command can only restore the most recent change you made; previous changes are lost.

The *named buffers* and *numbered buffers* are useful for moving blocks of text around a file, or between different files. In Chapter 8, for example, you will move six lines of text from one place in a file to another. You will do this by positioning the cursor at the beginning of the block of text and issuing the command

```
"a6yy
```

This is best understood when read backwards: **yy** stands for "yank," which means in this case "copy"; the 6 refers to six lines of text; and "a (double quote-a) specifies a particular named buffer. Therefore, this command tells **vi** to copy six lines of text and place them in the named buffer "a.

To retrieve the text from the named buffer, you place the cursor where you want it, and type the command

```
"ap
```

which tells **vi** to "put" a copy of the contents of the named buffer "a into the work buffer.

Remember that buffers are only *temporary* storage locations; their contents are lost once you leave **vi**.

Spell and Look

For the benefit of people who occasionally misspell words, UNIX offers the **spell** utility. (Strictly speaking, **spell** is not a part of **vi**, but we'll discuss it here because you'll most often use **spell** and **vi** together.) **spell** goes through a file and checks every word against the UNIX word list (sometimes called a "dictionary"). When **spell** encounters words or group of characters that are not on the word list, it displays them on the screen.

Although **spell** is very useful, it has its limitations. It cannot detect grammatical errors or words used incorrectly. Thus if you wrote "up" when you meant "down," or "wait" instead of "weight," **spell** cannot help you.

A related utility, **look**, allows you to look up words in the list that is used by **spell**. You will learn how to use both **look** and **spell** in Chapter 8.

Exercises

(1)   Define (a) text editor; (b) buffer; (c) cursor; (d) work buffer; (e) named buffer; (f) unnamed buffer; (g) yank; (h) put.

(2)   Specify which **vi** mode you would use to (a) delete a line; (b) yank a line; (c) write over old text; (d) move the cursor; (e) add text to a new line above the current cursor position.

(3)   How do you get from the **vi** command mode to the insert mode? How do you get back again?

(4)   What do the UNIX commands shown below do?
      (a)   `look pre` `RET`
      (b)   `spell file1` `RET`
      (c)   `vi file2` `RET`

(5)   Describe what happens when the following **vi** commands are given:
      (a)   `"z10yy`
      (b)   `"kp`
      (c)   `u`

7. Tutorial: Editing with vi

In this chapter, you will see how to use the **vi** editor to create and edit a new file. If you haven't already done so, log in and set your terminal. Then follow the examples.

Opening a New File

Begin by creating a new file named *poems*. Simply type the command

```
$vi poems RET
```

If your terminal is set properly,* you should see something like

```
□
~
~
~
~
~
~
~
~
~
~
~
"poems" [new file]
```

The tildes (~) are used to mark empty lines in the work buffer. The box on the first line represents the cursor, which shows the point at which any new text would be entered (the actual appearance of the cursor depends on the particular type of terminal you are using).

---

* Unless your terminal is set up correctly, it will not work as it should. If you forgot to specify the terminal type when you logged in, UNIX will probably assume that you have an old-style "dumb" terminal, and it will respond with the message

```
[Using open mode]
"poems" [new file]
```

It is a good idea to exit the editor and set the terminal type before proceeding. To exit **vi** without creating a new file, type

```
:q! RET
```

Set your terminal type, then start this chapter over again.

Inserting Text

Now enter text into the work buffer using the **i** ("insert ") command. Type

    i

This command does not appear on the screen, but everything you type subsequently will. Try typing in the following lines of verse (ignore any mistakes for now—you'll see how to correct them later):

    Mary had a little lamb, RET
    A little cheese, RET
    A little ham. RET
    Burp !

Although these lines appear on the terminal screen, they are not yet saved in the file. Remember, you must "write" these lines from the buffer into the file to save them. First, press ESCAPE to get back into the command mode:

    ESC

Now give the "write" command, which is done by typing a colon (:), a *w*, and a RETURN. Note that the cursor jumps to the bottom of the screen when you type the colon:

    :w RET

The computer will respond with a message such as

    "poems" [New file] 4 lines, 61 characters

Leave the file using the "quit" command:

    :q RET

The computer will answer with the shell prompt to let you know you are no longer in **vi**, but are back in the UNIX shell:

    $

Moving the Cursor

Reopen the file you have just created. This is done by typing the command

    $vi poems RET

You should see something like

```
Mary had a little lamb,
A little cheese,
A little ham.
Burp!
~
~
~
~
~
"poems" 4 lines, 61 characters
```

The cursor is positioned over the first character in the work buffer. You will want to make some changes in this text, which will require that you move the cursor around the file. Moving the cursor is done in the command mode. (If you aren't sure which mode you're in, just hit the ESCAPE key to get into the command mode.) If your terminal has arrow keys (often called *cursor-control keys*), you might be able to use them to move the cursor one space at a time. Their meaning should be obvious:

These keys do not always work as they should on some types of terminals. In the command mode, the h, j, k, and l keys act the same as the arrow keys:

h	move one space left
j	move one space down
k	move one space up
l	move one space right

Pressing the SPACE bar or BACKSPACE key moves the cursor right or left, respectively, along the line:

SPACE	move one space right
BACK	move one space left

To move to the start of a neighboring line, use the RETURN key or minus sign (-):

RET	move to beginning of next line down
–	move to beginning of previous line

Each of these cursor-control commands moves the cursor one space or one line at a time. On many terminals, holding a key down causes its function to be repeated rapidly. This can be useful when you want to move quickly through the file.

Practice using the various cursor-control keys until you get a feel for how they work.

Replacing Text

The first change to the file *poems* will be to replace *Burp* with something more suitable (Mary is very polite and would never burp at the dinner table). Move the cursor down to the fourth line and position it over the *B* in *Burp*. Now type

```
R
Delicious!
```

The initial *R* (for "Replace") does not appear on the screen, but it does take **vi** from the command mode into the insert mode. *Delicious!* is written right over the offending *Burp*. Return to the command mode, and write the changes into the file with the command

$\boxed{\text{ESC}}$:w $\boxed{\text{RET}}$

The result is

```
Mary had a little lamb,
A little cheese,
A little ham.
Delicious!
~
~
~
~
~
~
"poems" 4 lines, 66 characters
```

The cursor should remain over the last character you typed (the exclamation point, "!").

Adding Text

Next, use the **a** ("add") command to add text to the file. Just type

```
a
```

Note that this command does not appear on the screen. Now type the following lines (hit RETURN at the end of each line to start a new line):

$\boxed{\text{RET}}$
```
Mary had a polar bear
Whose fur was white as snow,
And everywhere that big bear went
The people let it go.
```

Hit ESCAPE to get back into the command mode:

$\boxed{\text{ESC}}$

You are finished with this file for now, so try the **q** ("quit") command:

```
:q RET
```

The computer will respond with the message

```
No write since last change (:q! overrides)
```

This means you have not written the additional text into the file yet. (Remember, just because it appears on the screen does not mean it is in the file.) Typing

```
:wq RET
```

writes the changes into the file and gets you out of the editor. The result should be something like this:

```
Mary had a little lamb,
A little cheese,
A little ham.
Delicious!
Mary had a polar bear
Whose fur was white as snow,
And everywhere that big bear went
The people let it go.
~
~
~
"poems" 8 lines, 174 characters
$
```

The prompt ($) indicates that you are back in the UNIX shell.

Opening Lines and Inserting Text

Two more insert commands are frequently useful:

    o   open a new line below the current line, and move the cursor there

    O   Open a new line above the current line, and move the cursor there

To see how these are used, reopen the file *poems*. The cursor should be positioned initially on the first line. Now type an uppercase *O*:

```
O
```

Note that the existing text moved down one space, leaving the cursor on a blank line. Next type

```
TAB  Poem #1
ESC
```

Pressing ESCAPE puts you back in the command mode, allowing you to move around the file. Move the cursor down to the line containing the word *Delicious* and type the open command using the lowercase *o*:

o

This creates an open line below *Delicious* and places the cursor there. Everything below the new line is shifted downward. Now type

| RET |
| TAB | Poem #2
| ESC | :wq | RET |

The result should be

```
        Poem #1
Mary had a little lamb,
A little cheese,
A little ham.
Delicious!

        Poem #2
Mary had a polar bear
Whose fur was white as snow,
And everywhere that big bear went
The people let it go.
~
~
~
"poems" 11 lines, 193 characters
§
```

Correcting Your Mistakes

Everyone makes an occasional error, so **vi** thoughtfully provides several means of correcting mistakes. These commands work only in the command mode. (When in doubt, hit ESCAPE to get into the command mode.)

x	delete one character
dd	delete entire line
u	undo most recent change
:q!	quit without saving changes

To delete a single character, move the cursor over that character and press the *x* key. To delete an entire line, type *dd*. To delete *n* lines (where *n* is any positive integer), move the cursor to the first of the lines to be deleted and type *ndd*.

If you make a change and then think better of it, you can undo the most recent change by the command

ESC u RET

If you make too many changes to undo with this command, you can always use the command

ESC :q! RET

which quits the text editor without saving any changes.

Summary

You have learned to use a number of the most important **vi** commands, which are listed below. Note that the commands beginning with a colon (:) appear at the bottom of the screen and must be followed by RETURN. Also note that none of the other commands given in the **vi** command mode appear on the screen as you type them.

Opening, Writing, and Closing Files (use RETURN)

vi *file*	open file *file* (UNIX shell command)
:w	write changes into file
:q	quit **vi**
:wq	write changes into file and quit **vi**
:q!	quit without writing changes into file

Inserting Text (vi command mode)

a	add text to the right of the current cursor location
i	insert text to the left of the cursor
O	open up a new line above the current line
o	open up a new line below the current line
R	replace (type over) text
ESC	return to command mode

Moving the Cursor (vi command mode)

←↓↑→	move one space in direction indicated
h	move one space left
j	move one space down
k	move one space up
l	move one space right
SPACE	move one space right
BACK	move one space left
RET	move to beginning of next line down
–	move to beginning of previous line

Correcting Mistakes (vi command mode)

x	delete one character
dd	delete entire line
ndd	delete *n* lines
u	"undo" most recent change

Exercises

The exercises marked with an asterisk (*) are to be done at the terminal.

(1)   What does the message "[Using open mode]" mean?

(2)*   If there are any typos in your file *poems,* use the **vi** editor to correct them.

(3)*   The **vi** command **J** ("join") allows you to join two lines together. To try it out, use the editor to create a file named *try.vi*, and enter the following lines into the file:

```
This sentence was
split in two.
```

Press ESCAPE to put **vi** into the command mode, then move the cursor up to the first line and type a J. What happens? What is the difference between the **j** and **J** commands? (Leave the file open; you will want to use it for the next exercise.)

(4)*   You have already seen how the **vi** command **a** allows you to insert text to the right of the current cursor position. The command **A** is also used to insert text, but at the end of the current line. Try it: in the file *try.vi*, type an *A* and enter the following

```
This demonstrates the A command.
```

Press ESCAPE to put **vi** back into the command mode. (There is no reason to save this file, so quit the editor *without* writing the file onto disk.)

(5)*   Using the **vi** editor, create a new file named *747art* and type in the following quote, making sure that you press RETURN each time the cursor nears the right edge of the screen:

It is hard to deny, yet rarely said, that the creative impulse was redirected at some point early in this century, or perhaps in the 19th, away from some of its normal artistic channels and into new ones associated with engineering and technology. Quite apart from being useful, a Boeing 747 is a far more impressive aesthetic object than what passes for "art" in our contemporary museums.

--Tom Bethell

Make sure to write this into the file before you quit the **vi** editor. (Bonus question: Do you agree with Mr. Bethell?)

(6)*   Most computer terminals have a useful feature called *wraparound*. Try an experiment to find out whether your terminal does:

(a) Open a new file *wrap* and begin typing in the quote by Tom Bethell, only this time do *not* press RETURN when the cursor reaches the end of the screen. Instead, keep typing and observe what happens. If the cursor automatically moves down to the next line as you type, your terminal has wraparound—it *wraps* a long line around to the next line to fit it on the screen. If, on the other hand, the cursor remains at the end of the line as you type, your terminal lacks wraparound.

(b) Continue typing in the entire Bethell quote without pressing the RETURN key. (This may be a bit difficult if your terminals does not have the wraparound feature, but do the best you can.) Write the quote into the file and quit the **vi** editor.

(c) Reopen the file *wrap.* How many lines and characters do you see on the screen? How many lines and characters does the editor say are in the file? (Moral #1: What you see on the screen is not necessarily what you get in the file. Moral #2: If you want to start a new line, press RETURN—don't rely on the wraparound.)

8. Tutorial: More vi Editing

You learned enough about the **vi** editor in the previous chapter to create and edit files. Now you'll see some additional features that can be very useful.

Using spell

spell is a UNIX utility that checks your spelling. To see how **spell** works, introduce a few misspelled words into **the file** *poems* that you created in the last chapter. Log in and set your terminal type. Then **use vi** to open *poems*:

```
$vi poems RET
```

Using the **R** ("replace") **command,** make some changes in the poems (underlined words):

```
        Poem #1
Marye had a wittle wamb,
A wittle cheese,
A wittle ham.
Delisious!

        Poem #2
Mary had a polar beer
Whose fir was white as snow,
And everywhere that big bare went
The people let it go.
~
~
```

Write these changes to the **file and** quit the editor:

```
ESC wq RET
```

Now type

```
$spell poems RET
```

spell responds with a list **of words:**

```
Delisious
Marye
wamb
wittle
```

Note that although *wittle* appears three times in the file, it is listed only once by **spell.** Note too that **spell** caught the unusual spelling of Mary; the word list includes many proper names. But **spell** missed some words: *beer*, *fir*, and *bare*. The reason is simple: these are legitimate words in **spell**'s **word** list. Remember, **spell** does not really check for spelling errors; rather, it looks for **groups** of characters that do not match those in its word list. Consequently, it will not **detect words** that are used out of context.

Looking up Words

If you are unsure of the spelling of a word, you can use **look**. Suppose you wanted to know how to spell *relief*. Is it "*i* before *e*" or "*e* before *i*"? Try the following command:

        $look relief RET

The computer will respond with

        relief

indicating that this matches a word on its list. On the other hand, type

        $look releif RET

and the computer responds with the system prompt only, since there is no word *releif* in the word list:

        $

To see all the words on the list starting with *rel,* type

        $look rel RET

Finding Text

The **vi** editor can locate particular words or groupings of characters anywhere in the file. This is useful when correcting spelling errors. For example, **spell** identified the misspelled word *Delisious* in the file *poems*. To find this word, open the file and type a slash (/) followed by the misspelling:

        /Delisious RET

This will appear at the bottom of the screen, then the cursor will move to the place where the word is located. You may then use **vi**'s editing commands to correct the spelling. If you suspect that the same misspelling also appears elsewhere, type (from the command mode, of course)

        / RET

If the computer can find no other instances of this word, it will respond

        Pattern not found

It is also possible to search backward through a file from the current cursor location using a question mark (?) instead of the slash (/):

        ?wittle RET

This will find one of the occurrences of the word *wittle*. To check for the next occurrence type

? RET

Take time now to find and correct the errors you introduced into the file *poems*. Remember to write the changes into the file before quitting the editor.

Jumping around the File

The **vi** editor provides a convenient way to jump to a specified line of the file. To see how this is done, open up the file *poems*, and while still in the command mode, type

        7G

in which the *G* stands for "Go." To go all the way to the bottom of the file, type the command

        G

To jump back 9 lines from your current position, type a 9 and a minus sign (–):

        9–

Similarly, you can jump forward 5 lines from your current position using the command

        5+

Setting Line Numbers

Of course, if you are to be jumping forward or backward to specific lines, it would be helpful to number the lines. In the command mode, type the line

        :set nu RET

This causes line numbers to be placed down the left-hand margin:

```
 1      Poem #1
 2    Mary had a little lamb,
 3    A little cheese,
 4    A little ham.
 5    Delicious!
 6
 7      Poem #2
 8    Mary had a polar bear
 9    Whose fur was white as snow,
10    And everywhere that big bear went
11    The people let it go.
```

The line numbers that appear on the screen are not written into the file; they disappear as soon as the file is closed. If you want to remove the numbers without closing the file, type

```
ESC :set nonu RET
```

Yanking and Putting

Occasionally, you may need to move large blocks of text around within a file or between files. To see how this is done, use **vi** to open the file *poems*. The cursor should be positioned over the first letter (the *P* in *Poem*). Next, copy six lines into a named buffer, which is done by typing the following command (no RETURN is required):

```
"a6yy
```

This means "yank six lines of text and place them in the named buffer "a." The command itself does not appear on the screen, but the computer usually puts a message at the bottom of the screen:

```
6 lines yanked
```

Now move the cursor down to the last line in the file and type

```
"ap
```

which means "take a copy of contents of the named buffer "a and *put* them here." The first six lines of Poem #1 should appear. The computer will also tell you how many lines were placed:

```
6 lines
```

The contents of the named buffer are not changed; you can put another six lines into the text. To do this, move the cursor down to the last line of the file and type

```
"ap
```

The first six lines of Poem #1 should appear again. You could keep this up all day, but for now just write and quit:

```
:wq RET
```

It is important to remember that buffers are only *temporary* storage locations; their contents are lost once you quit **vi**. Check this yourself by reopening the file *poems* and trying the **put** command you used before:

```
$vi poems RET
"ap
```

The computer will respond with a message such as

```
Nothing in register a
```

Leave the file open; you'll need it in the next section.

Moving Text between Files

The named and numbered buffers are also used to transfer text from one file to another. Suppose you want to copy the first six lines of *poems* into a new file. The first step is to **yank** these lines into a named buffer:

```
"m6yy
```

The computer will respond

```
6 lines yanked
```

Now type the command

```
:e stuff RET
```

This tells the editor that you want to work on the file *stuff*. Since there is no file named *stuff*, the editor opens an empty work buffer:

```
□
~
~
~
~
~
~
~
"stuff" No such file or directory
```

Now put the lines from the named buffer "m with the command

```
"mp
```

You should see something like this

```
     Poem #1
M ary had a little lamb,
A little cheese,
A little ham.
Delicious!

~
~
6 lines
```

Finally, write these lines into the file and quit the editor:

ESC :wq RET

The editor will tell you the size of the new file that you just created:

```
"stuff" [New file] 6 lines, 77 characters
```

Summary

You must press RETURN after a **spell** command, and after each **vi** command that begins with a slash (/), question mark (?), or colon (:). None of the other commands listed here requires a RETURN.

Check Spelling (UNIX shell commands)

spell *file*	list misspelled words found in *file*
look *word*	look for *word* in UNIX word list
look *pre*	look for words in UNIX word list beginning with *pre*

Search for Word (vi command mode)

/*word*	search forward through the file for the first occurrence of *word*
/	continue search for the next occurrence of *word*
?*word*	search backward through the file for the first occurrence of *word*
?	continue search backward for the next occurrence of *word*

Jump to Line (vi command mode)

n+	jump forward (down) *n* lines
n−	jump backward (up) *n* lines
*n*G	Go to line number *n*
G	Go to the bottom of the file

Line Numbers (vi command mode)

:set nu	set line numbers on the screen
:set nonu	remove line numbers

Yank and Put (vi command mode)

"k*n*yy	yank (copy) *n* lines into buffer "k
"kp	put the contents of buffer "k below the current line

Edit Another File (vi command mode)

:e *file*	edit *file*

Exercises

(1)* Use **spell** on the files that you created in the previous chapters. If **spell** reports an error in a file, open that file and use the search command to find the misspelled words. Make the necessary corrections.

(2)* Use **look** to determine whether the following are found in the UNIX word list: (a) your first name; (b) your last name; (c) the last name of the Vice President; (d) Kabul, the capital of Afghanistan; (e) *herpetologist;* (f) *ornithology.*

(3)* One of the requirements for a good UNIX password is that it not be a common word or name. Some UNIX installations will not accept any word in the internal word list. Use **look** to see whether your password is listed.

(4)* In a previous exercise, you created a file named *747art.* Open this file and use the search commands to locate the sentence beginning with the word *Quite.* Yank the lines that contain this entire sentence. (You may have to take a few words from the preceding sentence as well.) Use the **edit** command to transfer these lines to a new file *art.*

(5)* Your file *poems* should now contain several copies of Poem #1. Open the file and delete the second and third copy. Then use the **edit** command to transfer Poem #2 to the file *stuff.* The two files should now contain the same text.

Part IV
UNIX COMMUNICATIONS

9. UNIX Communications

In this chapter, you will learn about networking of computers. You will also learn about various programs that allow you to communicate with other computer users, including electronic mail.

Local Area Networks

A *network* is a group of computers that are interconnected to share information and resources. Computer networks are often classified according to size and geographical coverage.

A *Local Area Network* or *LAN* consists of computers that are close to one another—typically in the same building. A common way to link computers in a LAN is with Ethernet, which uses coaxial cables similar to those used by cable television. The advantage of Ethernet is that it allows very rapid transfer of data. (However, the special cables and connectors tend to be quite expensive.)

Wide Area Networks

Different LANs can be linked together to form larger networks. This usually requires a computer called a *gateway* to handle signals between the networks. Occasionally you will hear the terms *Campus* (or *Company*) *Area Network (CAN)* or *Metropolitan Area Network (MAN)* used to describe these networks.

Larger still are the *Wide-Area Networks* (*WANs*), which can span continents. A WAN may use long-distance telephone lines, microwave links, or communications satellites. Some of the larger networks are listed below:

- **ARPAnet.** This is one of the oldest networks in the United States. It was set up by the Advanced Research Projects Agency (ARPA) to support projects sponsored by the Department of Defense. ARPAnet has been interconnected with other government networks to form the Internet (see below).

- **NSFnet.** This is an international network operated by the National Science Foundation. It connects several hundred universities and research institutions. It is now part of the Internet.

- **Internet.** This is a huge international network that was created in 1982 by interconnecting three major government networks (ARPAnet, Milnet, and NSFnet). It is now connected to more than a thousand other networks around the world. Internet permits users to exchange electronic mail, to transfer files, and to log in and work on remote machines.

- **USENET.** Begun in 1979 as an "electronic bulletin board" for sharing information between two universities in North Carolina, USENET has grown into a decentralized network connecting more than 200,000 UNIX users worldwide. USENET is best known for its electronic news groups.

- **BITNET.** The name is short for "Because It's Time Network." BITNET was started at the City University of New York (CUNY) in 1981. It has since expanded to include more than 2000 computers around the world. BITNET handles electronic mail, terminal-to-terminal messages, and file transfers.

- **uucp**. The name **uucp** is short for "UNIX to UNIX copy." This is not really a network, but rather a set of programs designed for distributing UNIX software updates over ordinary long-distance telephone lines. However, some people do talk of the **uucp** network.

Your system may not have access to all of these networks; ask your system administrator for more details.

LAN Addresses

To communicate with someone who has an account on the same computer you are using, all you have to know is the other person's login name. However, to communicate with someone on a different machine, you have to be able to specify the network address.

The computers making up the network are called *hosts* or *nodes*, and each has its own *host name* or *node name*. To address a user on another machine on your LAN, you need to know the user's login and the machine's node name. There are two common ways to express this address. The first, which is used with **uucp**, lists the host name first, followed by the user's login. The host name and login are separated by an exclamation mark (often called a *bang*):

host!user

Suppose, for example, that you want to address something to *fred*, who has an account on the machine *admin*. Using the **uucp** style, his address would be

admin!fred

The other method of forming an address is the *Internet style*, which puts the user's login name before the host machine's name. An "at" symbol (@) separates the login name and the host name:

user@host

Using the Internet style, *fred* on the machine *admin* would have the address

fred@admin

Which convention you use—**uucp** or Internet—depends on how your LAN is set up, although the Internet style is perhaps the more common. You should ask your system administrator which to use.

WAN Addresses

The conventions for addressing another user over a WAN are similar to those for the LAN, but more information is required. Most of the large networks use Internet addresses. In addition to the user's login and the host name, you must include the *domain*, which typically indicates the name and type of institution that owns that host computer :

user@host.domain

Suppose, for example, that you want to address something to *jpjones*, who has an account on the machine *host1*, which is located at Podunk State University. The Internet address might look something like

> ***jpjones@host1.podunkst.edu***

The domain in this case is ***podunkst.edu***. The *edu* ending indicates that ***podunkst*** is an educational institution. The common domain endings are

> *.com* ⇒ commercial organization
>
> *.edu* ⇒ educational institution
>
> *.gov* ⇒ government agency
>
> *.mil* ⇒ military agency
>
> *.org* ⇒ nonprofit organization

Electronic Mail

The most frequently used communications facility is *electronic mail*, sometimes called *E-mail*, which allows you to exchange messages with other users.

The basic AT&T E-mail utility is called, appropriately enough, **mail**. A somewhat more elaborate utility, also called **mail**, is found on Berkeley UNIX. Most AT&T systems also offer **mailx**, which is essentially the same as the Berkeley utility. Your system may have other E-mail utilities as well. However, since almost all UNIX systems offer either Berkeley **mail** or AT&T **mailx**, we will concentrate on these two utilities.

You will learn more about **mailx** and **mail** in the next chapter.

write and talk

The **write** and **talk** utilities are similar in that both allow you to communicate directly with a user who is logged into the system. Whatever either of you types on your keyboard appears simultaneously on both screens. Of the two utilities, **write** is less convenient because the messages can become garbled if both of you try to type at the same time. **talk** separates the messages, even if both of you type simultaneously. Using either utility is a five-step process:

(1) The first user requests a session with the second user. Suppose, for example, that the user *george* wishes to communicate with *martha*. To do this, he would type

> $talk martha RET

or

> $write martha RET

(2) The second user is notified. Thus if *martha* is logged in and receiving messages, she will be alerted:

```
        Message from george...
```

(3)   The second user agrees to answer. *martha* would have to type

$talk george RET

or

$write george RET

(4)   The two users exchange messages. Anything that either user types will be displayed on both terminals. Most people using **write** work out a convention whereby only one types at a time, signaling the end of a thought with an *o* (for "over").

(5)   When finished, they break off communication. To quit **talk**, one of the parties has to type CONTROL+c. To quit *write*, however, *both* must type CONTROL+d.

By the way, you can refuse to accept **write** or **talk** messages with the command

```
$mesg n
```

which is short for "messages—no." Anyone trying to establish contact with you using **write** or **talk** will get the message:

```
Your party is refusing messages.
```

(Electronic mail will still get through, however.) To accept messages again, you would use the command

```
$mesg y
```

finger

The **finger** command tells you the real name of the person that uses a particular login name. Suppose, for example, that you want to know who *aadams* is. You would type

$finger aadams RET

You might see something like this on the screen:

```
Login name: aadams          In real life: Abigail Adams
112 Independence Hall       Phone: 555-1776
```

Remote Operations

It is not uncommon for a user to have accounts on several different machines on a network. If you do, you may log into one machine, and from there perform various *remote operations* involving the other machine(s). Some of these are

- **rlogin** ("remote login") allows you to log into a remote UNIX system from the account you are presently using. You have to have an account and a password on the remote machine.

- **telnet** also allows you to log into a remote machine. It can be used to communicate with either UNIX or non-UNIX hosts.

- **rcp** ("remote copy") allows you to copy files from one host to another over the network. **rcp** works much like **cp**, except with **rcp** you must supply the names of the hosts as well as the pathnames of the files themselves.

- **ftp** ("File-Transfer Program") was designed for transferring files over the ARPAnet. Unlike **rcp**, **ftp** works with UNIX or non-UNIX hosts.

- **rwho** ("remote who") lists the users who are currently logged into your LAN. For each user, **rwho** lists the login name, the name of the machine, the terminal being used, and the date and time the user logged in.

- **ruptime** ("remote up-time") shows the current status of the machines attached to your LAN, whether they are working ("up") or not ("down"), how many users are logged in, etc. This can be helpful when you want to find a computer that is not too heavily used.

If you are interested, you can use the **man** command to find out more about these operations. (The **man** command and the UNIX manual are described in Appendix A.)

News

One of the most entertaining—and informative—features of the USENET is the electronic news service. Ask your system administrator about the local policy regarding access to the network news.

Exercises

(1)   Define: (a) network; (b) LAN; (c) CAN; (d) WAN; (e) gateway; (f) host; (g) node; (h) E-mail.

(2)   Is your computer part of a network? If so, how many other machines are connected to the same network? Where are they located?

(3)   Does your system have access to a WAN? If so, what is the Internet address of your computer?

(4)   Does your system permit access to the network news services? If so, what is the command for reading the news?

10. Tutorial: Using Electronic Mail

One of the most frequently used features of the UNIX operating system is *electronic mail* or *E-mail*, which allows you to send and receive messages. In this chapter, you will see how to use Berkeley UNIX's **mail** or AT&T UNIX's **mailx**.

Sending Electronic Mail

If you are just getting started with a brand-new UNIX account, it is unlikely that anyone has sent you E-mail yet. However, you can start by sending yourself a message. If you are using AT&T UNIX, type in the following line (using your login in place of *login*):

$mailx *login* RET

If you are using BSD UNIX, type (using your login in place of *login*):

$mail *login* RET

Either way, the computer will ask you for the subject of the message. Type in an appropriate title and press RETURN:

Subject: Test Message #1 RET

Now type the body of the message itself. The mail program has only limited editing capabilities: you can edit only one line at a time, and you cannot go back to edit a previous line. Therefore, make sure each line is correct before hitting RETURN to start a new line. When you are finished with the entire message, press RETURN, then CONTROL+d (for *done*):

Don't be alarmed. RET
This is only a test. RET
CTRL + d

The computer will ask if you want to send carbon copies (Cc) to anyone. For now, just press RETURN. The UNIX prompt tells you that you are back in the UNIX shell:

Cc: RET
$

To summarize, the process of sending E-mail to someone is

(1) Type *mailx* or *mail*, followed by the login of the person to whom you want the message sent. Then press RETURN.

(2) The computer will prompt you for a title (Subject) for the message. Type it in and press RETURN.

(3) Now type the message itself. When you are finished, type RETURN, then CONTROL+d.

(4) The computer will prompt you for the logins of persons to whom you would send copies of the message. If there are none, simply press RETURN. The computer responds with the shell prompt to indicate that you are back in the shell.

See if you can do this on your own. Try sending "Test Message #2" to yourself.

Mailing a File

Because the mail program has only limited editing capabilities, it is usually more convenient to make up a file using the **vi** editor, and then redirect the file into the mail program. Try sending a copy of the file *poems* to yourself (use your own login name in place of *login*):

> \$mailx *login* < poems RET

or

> \$mail *login* < poems RET

Note the redirection arrow (<); it tells the mail program to take as input the contents of the file **poems**.

Reading Your Mail

You have just sent three messages to yourself. To read your mail, type in the **mailx** or **mail** command without specifying a login name:

> \$mailx RET   or   \$mail RET

The system will respond with a list of the messages. The three messages you have just sent yourself should be listed. The first new message on the list will be marked by a >:

```
>N 1 yourlogin Thu Nov 22 15:27 11/321 "Test Message #1"
 N 2 yourlogin Thu Nov 22 15:35 11/321 "Test Message #2"
 N 3 yourlogin Thu Nov 22 15:42 20/442
&
```

The > in the first column points to the current message. An *N* indicates a new message. The messages are numbered (1 through 3 in this case). The login name of the sender is shown, along with the date and time the message was received and the number of lines and characters the message contains (lines/characters). Finally, the subject of the message is given in quotes.

The ampersand (&) on the last line is the *mail prompt*. It tells you that the mail program is awaiting your instructions. Some systems use a question mark (?) as a prompt.

If you wish to read one of the messages, simply type in its number after the prompt and press RETURN. To see the second message, for example, type a *2* and then RETURN:

```
&2 RET
```

This will cause the second message to appear:

```
Message 2:
From yourlogin Day Month Time Year
Date: Day Month Time Year
From: yourlogin (Your name)
To: (Your login name)
Subject: Test Message #2

Don't be alarmed. This is only a test.
&
```

The mail program places some additional lines at the top of your message before sending it on. These lines make up the *mail header*, which contains such information as the name, the login, and the address of the person who sent the message. Note that you cannot send an anonymous mail message!

Once you have read the message, there are a number of things you can do with it. Without leaving the mail program, you can reply to the message, save it in a file, or delete it.

Replying to a Message

It is a good idea to respond promptly to any E-mail that you receive. While you are still in the mail program, use the **R** ("Reply") command:

```
&R2
```

This tells the mail program that you want to reply to the user who sent the second message.* The mail program will take care of addressing your reply; it even fills in the "Subject" for you. All you have to do is type the message, hitting RETURN and CONTROL+d at the end of the message:

```
Subject: Re: Test Message #2

What a relief. RET
CTRL + d
```

Saving and Deleting Messages

You can also save a message in a file with the **s** ("save") command. To save the first message in a new file *message1*, type

```
&s1 message1 RET
```

---

* If you type a lowercase *r*, your reply will go not only to the person who sent the original message, but also to everyone who received a carbon copy of the original. Note that some systems reverse this: **r** is the command to respond to the sender of the original message, while **R** sends a copy of your response to the sender and all recipients of the original message.

This creates a new file in your home directory named *message1*, and places in it the text of the message, *including the mail header*. (If you already have a file named *message1* in your home directory, the message is appended to the file.) The original message is deleted from your mailbox.

Deleting a Message

You can delete a message that you don't wish to save. To delete the third message, type

&d3 RET

Quitting mailx or mail

You can get out of either **mailx** or **mail** with the **q** ("quit") command

&q RET

Any unread mail will remain in your mailbox.

Using vi inside mail

As we said before, the mail program has only limited editing capabilities. However, you can use **vi** to edit messages while you are still inside the mail program. To see how this works, start an E-mail message to yourself:

$mailx *yourlogin* RET   or $mail *yourlogin* RET

Specify a subject, then type a short message, such as

```
There once was a fellow named Chester,
Whose knowledge grew lesser and lesser.
It at last grew so small,
He knew nothing at all;
So they hired him as a professor.
```

When you have finished, start a new line, and at the beginning of the line type a tilde (~) followed by a *v* (for **vi**), then RETURN:

RET
~v RET

This will bring up the **vi** editor and place your message in the buffer:

```
□
There once was a fellow named Chester,
Whose knowledge grew lesser and lesser.
It at last grew so small,
He knew nothing at all;
So they hired him as a professor.
~
~
~
~
"/tmp/Re24223 6 lines, 164 characters
```

Note that the cursor is placed at the top of the text. You can then use all of the familiar **vi** commands to edit the message. (Try it.) When you are finished, you can write the changes into the file and quit the editor:

$\boxed{\text{ESC}}$:wq $\boxed{\text{RET}}$

This will put you back in the mail program. You may see something like this:

```
(continue)
```

Now send the message in the usual way:

$\boxed{\text{RET}}$
$\boxed{\text{CTRL}}$ + $\boxed{\text{d}}$

You will be asked to specify carbon copies. For now, just press RETURN:

Cc: $\boxed{\text{RET}}$

This should get you out of the mail program:

$

Getting Help

Any time you forget what commands are used by **mailx** or **mail**, type the **?** ("help") command after the mail prompt. This will display a list of commands.

Getting the Address

Until now, you have been sending mail messages to yourself. Of course, there is not much point in doing this other than to see how it is done. You follow exactly the same procedure to send mail to someone else, except that you must address the message to their login name. That can be a problem when you do not know the proper login name.

If you can ask the person directly for his or her login, fine. Otherwise, you may have to make an intelligent guess at the login, and then use **finger** to confirm your guess. **finger** tells you the real name of the person that uses a particular login name. Try the **finger** command using your own login:

$finger *yourlogin* RET

We might see something like this on the screen:

```
Login name: yourlogin       In real life: Your Name
Your office                 Phone: 555-5555
```

However, if the **finger** command is not available, the system will say so:

```
finger: Command not found
```

Summary

Some of the commands discussed in this chapter are UNIX shell commands, others work only within **mailx** or **mail**. All of these commands must be terminated by a RETURN.

Reading Your Mail (UNIX shell commands)

mail	list messages received (Berkeley UNIX)
mailx	list messages received (AT&T System V UNIX)

Deleting, Saving, and Replying (**mailx** or **mail** commands)

d*n*	delete message number *n*
s*n file*	save message number *n* in *file*
R*n*	reply to person who sent message number *n*
r*n*	same as **R***n*, but also sends reply to everyone who received original

Note that on some systems, **R** and **r** are reversed: **R** is used to reply to everyone who received the original message; **r** is used to reply to the sender only.

Sending Mail (UNIX shell commands)

mail *xyz*	send message to *xyz* (Berkeley UNIX)
mailx *xyz*	send message to *xyz* (AT&T System V UNIX)

Mailing a File (UNIX shell commands)

mail *xyz* < *file*	mail the file *file* to the user *xyz* (Berkeley UNIX)
mailx *xyz* < *file*	mail the file *file* to the user *xyz* (AT&T UNIX)

Editing a Message Using vi (**mailx** or **mail** command)

~v	call up **vi** program to edit message

Identifying a User   (UNIX shell command)

`finger` *xyz* RET   get the real name of user with login *xyz*

Exercises

(1)*   Find someone with an account on your computer (or on the same network) and practice using **mailx** or **mail** to exchange messages.

(2)*   Find someone with an account on your computer (or on the same network) and practice using **write** or **talk** to exchange messages.

(3)*   The **s** command is used inside the mail program to save an E-mail message in a file. The **w** command also saves messages. Have someone send you E-mail (or send something to yourself), and use the **w** command to put it into a file. Exit the mail program, and examine the contents of the new file. What is the difference between **w** and **s**?

(4)*   Use the help command (**?**) inside the mail program to check on the commands that are available to you. What do the following commands do?

```
cd                  n                   top
d                   p                   u
e                   q                   v
f                   r                   x
h                   R                   z
m                   t                   z-
```

(5)*   The E-mail programs **mailx** and **mail** make use of *tilde escapes*. These are mail commands that begin with a tilde (~). You have seen how to use the tilde escape sequence *~v* to edit a message using the **vi** editor. Find out about other tilde escapes. First open up the mail program:

   `$mailx` *yourlogin* RET or `$mail` *yourlogin* RET

Specify a "Subject," then type the tilde escape sequence

   `~?` RET

to display a list of the tilde escapes. What do the following tilde escapes do?

```
~p
~h
~q
~r
~s
~x
```

Part V
THE UNIX SHELL

11. The UNIX Shell

The *shell* is the UNIX command processor. When you type a command and press RETURN, it is the shell that interprets the command and takes the appropriate action. In this chapter, we will take a closer look at how the shell works, and how you can make it work better for you.

Your Login Shell

There are three common UNIX shells available on most systems: the **Bourne Shell** (abbreviated **sh**), the **C Shell** (**csh**), and the **Korn Shell** (**ksh**). When your UNIX account was created, the system administrator selected a shell for you. This is called your *login shell*, because this is the shell you use each time you log in.

Once you have worked with the various shells available on your system, you may decide to change your login shell. Your system administrator can do this for you.*

Programs and Processes

This is a good place to point out the difference between a program and a process in UNIX jargon. A *program* is a set of coded instructions to the computer that is contained in a file. An example of a program is the **ls** command: it is just a sequence of computer instructions contained in the file */bin/ls*. Similarly, your login shell is also just another program residing in the directory */bin*.

A *process* is what you get whenever you tell the computer to run a program. Thus, when you issue the **ls** command, the computer looks in the file */bin/ls* and follows the program it finds there to create a process. Likewise, when you log in, the computer looks in the file containing the shell program and creates a shell process for you.

The important thing to remember is that there is only one copy of the **ls** program, but there may be many active **ls** processes. In the same way, there is only one copy of each shell program, but there may be many active shell processes.

Subshells

Your login shell starts up automatically when you log in. However, you are not limited to using this shell; you can easily call up another.

The **Bourne Shell** program is kept in the file */bin/sh*; to run this shell, simply type the command

$/bin/sh RET

Note that running a new shell this way does not change your login shell. Instead, your login shell "goes to sleep" while the new shell goes to work. The new shell is often called a *subshell* or *child shell*. When the subshell finishes its work, it "wakes up" the login shell, which takes over.

---

* Some systems allow you to change your own login shell using the **chsh** command.

The **Korn Shell** program is kept in the file */bin/ksh*. To run the **Korn Shell** as a subshell, type

$/bin/ksh`RET`

The **C Shell** program is kept in the file */bin/csh*. To run this shell as a subshell, type

$/bin/csh`RET`

To exit a subshell, and return to your login shell, use either the **exit** command or CONTROL+d:

$exit`RET`   or $`CTRL`+`d`

How the Shell Processes Commands

The entire process can be summarized this way:

(1)   The shell displays a prompt symbol on the screen to tell you it is ready.

(2)   You type in a command. As you type, the shell stores the characters and also echoes them back to the terminal screen.

(3)   You type RETURN. This is the signal for the shell to interpret the command and start working on it.

(4)   The shell looks for the appropriate software to run your command. If it can't find the right software, it gives you an error message. If it finds the right software, it asks the kernel to run it.

(5)   The kernel runs the requested software, signaling the shell when it is finished.

(6)   The shell again displays a prompt symbol.

Grouping Commands

Normally you type one command at a time, following each command by a RETURN, which is the signal for the shell to begin its work. However, it is possible to put multiple commands on the same line, if you separate the commands with semicolons. Thus the command line

$who; ls; cal`RET`

has the same effect as the three separate command lines

$who`RET`
$ls`RET`
$cal`RET`

Grouping and Redirection

Grouping several commands together can be especially useful when you want to redirect the output into a file. Consider, for example, the summer 1999 calendar you created in Chapter 4. You could make such a calendar in three steps:

```
$cal 6 1999 > summer99 RET
$cal 7 1999 >> summer99 RET
$cal 8 1999 >> summer99 RET
```

You could accomplish the same thing with just one line:

```
$(cal 6 1999; cal 7 1999; cal 8 1999) > summer99 RET
```

Note the parentheses; these are necessary to make sure the calendars for June, July, and August are all redirected into the same file. If the parentheses are omitted, the calendars for June and July will appear on the screen, and only the August calendar will be redirected into the file:

```
$cal 6 1999; cal 7 1999; cal 8 1999 > summer99 RET
```

Pipes and Tees

Suppose you wanted to display the calendars for the years 1999, 2000, and 2001, one right after the other. You could type the command

```
$cal 1999; cal 2000; cal 2001 RET
```

This will show the calendars, but they will scroll by so fast that you cannot read them. One way around this problem is to redirect the output into a file:

```
$(cal 1999; cal 2000; cal 2001) > temp RET
```

Now you can view the contents of *temp* using the **more** or **pg** utility:

```
$more temp RET          or      $pg temp RET
```

This will work, but it requires that you create a temporary file just to look at the output from the commands. You can avoid creating a file by using what is called a *pipe*, which connects the output from one utility to the input of another. In this case, we want to pipe the output of the **cal** utility to either **more** or **pg**. The pipe symbol is a vertical bar (|):

```
$(cal 1999; cal 2000; cal 2001) | more RET
```

or

```
$(cal 1999; cal 2000; cal 2001) | pg RET
```

Note how this differs from redirection with > or >>. Redirection places the output from a utility into a file; the piping operation directs the output to another utility.

A *tee* is like a pipe, except that it allows you to save output from one command in a file while it is piped to another command. Thus the command line

$(cal 2000; cal 2001) |tee calfile | more RET

places copies of the calendars for 2000 and 2001 into the file *calfile* as they are also displayed on the terminal screen by **more**.

Filters

A *filter* takes a stream of data from the standard input, transforms the data in some way, and sends the results to the standard output. Three commonly used UNIX filters are **sort**, **wc**, and **grep**, about which you will learn more in the next chapter.

Filters are often used with pipes and tees. Consider the **sort** command, which, as you might expect, sorts its input. Suppose you wanted to list, alphabetically by their login names, the users currently logged onto your machine. You could do this by piping the output from **who** into **sort**:

$who | sort RET

You can also give **sort** the name of a file to sort:

$sort poems RET

Wildcards

Typing and retyping file names can be a nuisance, especially if the names are long or there are very many of them. You can abbreviate file names using *wildcards*, which are characters that can stand for other characters (just as a joker in a pack of cards can stand for other cards in the pack). The wildcard symbols are the asterisk (*), the question mark (?), and the square brackets ([]).

The asterisk (*) is by far the most commonly used wildcard. It matches any character or string of characters, including blanks. Suppose, for example, that you had a directory named *Fun* containing the following files:

```
backgammon    backpacking   baseball      basketball
biking        blackjack     boxing        bridge
camping       canoeing      checkers      chess
crossword     dancing       eating        fencing
fishing       football      golf          hearts
hiking        karate        poker         rugby
sailing       skiing        softball      swimming
team1         team2         team3         team4
teamA         teamB         teamC         teamD
teamM         teamW         teamX         teamY
teamZ         track         wrestling
```

The directory *Fun* contains a large number of files. Using wildcards you can avoid having to list all of them when you are interested in just a few. For example, the command

```
$ls f*RET
```

will cause the shell to list only those files beginning in *f*:

```
fencing        fishing        football
```

The command

```
$ls *ballRET
```

will cause the shell to list the files that end in *ball:*

```
baseball       basketball     football       softball
```

You are not limited to using a single asterisk. For instance, the command

```
$ls *ack*RET
```

will list filenames that contain the sequence of letters *ack*

```
backgammon     backpacking    blackjack    track
```

The asterisk wildcard is very powerful, and must be used with care. The following command, for example, can erase all of the files in the current directory:

```
$rm *RET
```

The question mark (?) wildcard matches just one character at a time. For example,

```
$ls ?ikingRET
biking     hiking
```

The square brackets ([and]) are used to instruct the shell to match any characters that appear inside the brackets. For example

```
$ls team[ABXYZ] RET
teamA      teamB       teamX       teamY       teamZ
```

You can also indicate a range of characters, rather than list each character:

```
$ls team[1-4] RET
team1      team2       team3       team4
```

You can combine the wildcards *, ?, and []. Suppose you wanted to list all of the files in the directory *Fun* that begin with the letters *a*, *b*, or *c*. This command will do the trick:

```
$ls [abc]*RET
```

The bracketed letters tell the shell to look for any file names that have *a*, *b*, or *c* at the beginning. The asterisk matches any other sequence of letters. The result is

```
backgammon      backpacking     baseball    basketball
biking          blackjack       boxing      bridge
camping         canoeing        checkers    chess
crossword
```

Likewise, to list all of the files having names that end with any letter from *m* through *z*, you could use the command

$ls *[m-z] RET

The asterisk matches any sequence of characters; the brackets match only letters from *m* through *z* that appear at the end of the file name.

```
backgammon     checkers       chess          hearts
```

Quoting Special Characters

You will recall that UNIX file names should not contain any of the following special characters:

```
& * \ | [ ] { } $ < > ( ) # ? ' " / ; ^ !
```

By now it should be clear why: each of these characters has a special meaning to the shell. But sometimes this can be a problem. You may want to use a special character in its usual, everyday meaning. Consider, for example, the command line

$echo What time is it? RET

The shell will interpret the question mark as a wildcard, and it will try to find a file name to match it. Unless you happen to have a file with a three-character name beginning with *it*, the shell will not be able to find a match, and it will complain:

$echo: No match.

If you want the shell to treat a question mark as a question mark, not as a special character, you must *quote* it. One way to do this is to write a backslash (\) immediately before the question mark:

$echo What time is it\? RET

This produces the output

```
What time is it?
```

Note that the backslash does not appear in the output; its only purpose is to cancel the special meaning of the question mark.

The backslash only works on a single character. Thus, to produce the output

```
****Wake up!****
```

you would have to place a backslash in front of each of the special characters:

$echo ****Wake up\!**** RET

Having to quote each special character individually like this can be tedious. As an alternative, you can quote the entire string of characters all at once using single quotes:

$echo '****Wake up!****' RET

The single quotes (' . . . ') used here should not be confused with the single backquotes (` . . . `).* Backquotes, which are also called grave accent marks, are used to enclose commands that you want the shell to run. Thus, the command line

$echo It is now `date`. RET

will produce output that looks something like this

```
It is now Fri Aug 13 16:04:41 EST 1999.
```

where the shell has run the **date** utility and included the result in the output from **echo**. In contrast, this is what would happen if you left off the backquotes:

```
$echo It is now date. RET
It is now date.
```

Double quotes (" . . . ") are like single quotes but less powerful. Putting double quotes around a string of characters cancels the special meaning of any of the characters *except* the dollar sign ($), backquotes (` . . . `), or backslash (\).

The different ways of quoting special characters are summarized below:

\	Cancels the special meaning of the next character
' . . . '	Cancels the special meaning of any characters
" . . . "	Cancels the special meaning of any characters but $, ` . . . `, and \
` . . . `	Runs any commands in . . . ; output replaces ` . . . `

---

* Note that on some terminal screens, the single quote looks like an apostrophe ('), while the backquote looks like a single open quote ('). If you are confused by this, just try it a few times—the difference will become apparent.

Background Processing

As we said before, UNIX is a *multitasking* operating system, which means that it is capable of running more than one program for you at the same time. You can start a command and put it in the "background," to continue running while you work on another task in the foreground.

Running a background process is simple: type an ampersand (&) at the end of the command, before pressing RETURN. Consider a hypothetical long-running program called **longrun**. You could run this program in background and redirect the output into the file *longlist* with the command

    $*longrun* >longlist & RET

The shell assigns a *process-id number* (PID) to the job running in background (1216 in this example), then it displays a prompt:

    1216
    $

You can now enter another command, even if the **longrun** is not yet finished.

The PID is important if you want to stop a background job before it finishes. This is done with the **kill** command. To stop background process number 1216, you would use the command

    $kill 1216 RET

It is not a good idea to run a background process that requires interaction with the standard input or output, because this might conflict with the foreground process.

Exercises

(1)   Define: (a) shell; (b) subshell; (c) child shell; (d) program; (e) process; (f) pipe; (g) tee; (h) filter; (i) wildcard; (j) background; (k) PID.

(2)   What would each of the following commands do?
```
echo *
echo /*
echo \*
echo "*"
echo
echo */*
rm *   (Careful—do not try this!)
```

For Exercises 3–6, suppose your working directory contained the following files:

```
backgammon    backpacking   baseball      basketball
biking        blackjack     boxing        bridge
camping       canoeing      checkers      chess
crossword     dancing       eating        fencing
fishing       football      golf          hearts
hiking        karate        poker         rugby
sailing       skiing        softball      swimming
team1         team2         team3         team4
teamA         teamB         teamC         teamD
teamM         teamW         teamX         teamY
teamZ         track         wrestling
```

(3) How would you use **cat** to show contents of the files ending in *ing*?

(4) How would you list any files containing *x* or *X*? (In this case, *boxing* and *teamX*)?

(5) How would you show the contents of files with names containing *o*?

(6) How would you show the contents of the three files *backgammon*, *backpacking*, and *blackjack* using just one command?

12. Tutorial: Working with the Shell

In this chapter, you will practice grouping commands, running commands in the background, and using wildcards, pipes, tees, and filters.

Grouping Commands

Log in and set your terminal type. Then try grouping several commands on the same command line, using semicolons as separators between commands:

```
$who; cal; date RET
```

This should produce a list of the users currently logged into your system, the current month's calendar, and the current date and time. Next, try the same three commands, but redirect the output into the file *out1.tmp*:

```
$who; cal; date > out1.tmp RET
```

This command line should cause the list of users and current month's calendar to appear on the screen, as before, but the date and time should be redirected into the file *out1.tmp*. To check that this is what happened, use the **cat** command to examine the contents of *out1.tmp*:

```
$cat out1.tmp RET
```

Suppose you wanted to redirect the output from all three commands into a file. You could do this using the command line:

```
$who > out2.tmp; cal >> out2.tmp; date >> out2.tmp RET
```

This time, nothing appears on the screen except the prompt because the output from the commands was redirected into *out2.tmp*. Check this by using **cat** on *out2.tmp*:

```
$cat out2.tmp RET
```

Another way to redirect all three commands into the same file is to use parentheses to group them together. Try this command:

```
$(who; cal; date) > out3.tmp RET
$
```

Again, nothing appears on the screen except the prompt because the output from the commands was redirected into *out3.tmp*. Check this by using **cat** on *out3.tmp*

```
$cat out3.tmp RET
```

Wildcards

If you worked through the previous section carefully, you should now have three new files in your directory named *out1.tmp*, *out2.tmp*, and *out3.tmp*. You can (quickly) examine the contents of these three files using the command

```
$cat out* RET
```

This command will show all of the files having names that begin with *out*. Remember, the asterisk (*) is a wildcard that matches any character or string of characters. You could list all of the files ending in *.tmp* with the command

```
$cat *.tmp RET
```

You could also show the files *out1.tmp*, *out2.tmp*, and *out3.tmp* using the question mark wildcard (?), which matches any single character. Try this command:

```
$cat out?.tmp RET
```

The three files *out1.tmp*, *out2.tmp*, and *out3.tmp* differ only by one character—a number—and the question mark wildcard can stand for any of the numbers.

You won't be needing *out1.tmp*, *out2.tmp*, or *out3.tmp*, so let's remove them. This command will do the trick:

```
$rm out?.tmp RET
```

Pipes and Tees

Try this command line to list the root's subdirectories and their contents :

```
$ls /* RET
```

This will list the directories, but they will scroll by so fast that you cannot read them. One way around this difficulty is to pipe the output from **ls** to the **more** or **pg** utility:

```
$ls /* | more RET    or    $ls /* | pg RET
```

The vertical bar (|) is the pipe symbol.

You can use two pipes and a tee both to view the listing and to direct it into a file at the same time:

```
$ls /* | tee root.list | more RET
```

This places a list of the *root*, its children, and their contents into the file *root.list* as this list is also displayed on the terminal screen. Check that *root.list* does indeed contain the calendars:

```
$cat root.list RET
```

Using sort

The **sort** filter sorts its input. Use **sort** to list, alphabetically by their login names, the users currently logged onto your machine. Do this by piping the output from **who** into **sort**:

```
$who | sort RET
```

Next try **sort** on a file:

```
$sort poems RET
```

This will list on the screen the contents of the file *poems*, line by line according to the first character of the line. Note that lines starting with tabs are placed before those starting with the letter *A*:

```
        Poem #1
        Poem #2
A little cheese,
A little ham.
And everywhere that big bear went
Delicious!
Mary had a little lamb,
Mary had a polar bear
The people let it go.
Whose fur was white as snow,
```

Using wc

The **wc** ("word count") command counts the lines, words, and characters in its standard input. Thus the command

```
$wc poems RET
```

produces the output

```
11    38    192    poems
```

showing that there are 11 lines, 38 words, and 192 characters in the file *poems*. (To **wc**, a "word" is simply any group of characters followed by a blank or newline.) You can apply various options to the **wc** command so that it counts only the number of lines, or the number of words, or the number of characters. You can count the number of people logged into your system by piping the output from the **who** command through **wc**, using the **–l** option:

```
$who | wc -l RET
```

If there are five users logged in, the **who** command will produce five lines, one per user; **wc −l** then counts the number of lines, and returns the result:

    5

Using grep

Another useful filter is the **grep** utility, which searches line by line through its standard input looking for a *pattern*, which is just a sequence of characters that you specify. **grep** passes any line containing the desired pattern to the standard output. For instance, you could pipe the output from **who** though the **grep** command to see if a particular user is logged in. Try this command, putting your own login in place of *yourlogin*

    $who | grep *yourlogin* RET

In this case, *yourlogin* is the pattern that **grep** is looking for. If it finds a line containing this pattern, it will display that line on the screen:

    yourlogin ttyp0   Jul 10   10:33

The **grep** utility can also search through files for patterns. Thus, to search the file *poems* for lines containing the word *little*, you would use the command

    $grep little poems RET

Any lines containing the pattern are listed on the screen:

    A little cheese,
    A little ham.

Background Processing

As we said before, UNIX allows you to run a process in the "background," while you work on another task in the foreground. This is usually done for processes that take a long time to complete, and that don't write output to the terminal screen. As an example of such a long-running process, try the following

    $sleep 30 RET

The **sleep** command simply waits the specified number of seconds (in this case, 30 seconds) before returning to the shell. If you run **sleep** in the foreground, you cannot work on any other commands until the time is up; therefore, it is more common to run **sleep** in the background. Try this

    $(sleep 60; echo I am awake now) & RET
    3271
    $

In this example, the shell assigned a *process identification* (PID) number of 3271; the actual PID that you see will probably be different. The prompt indicates that you can now enter another command. Try the **ps** ("process status") command to check on what is happening:

    $ps RET

You might see something like this (although the PID numbers will be different):

```
PID   TTY   TIME  COMMAND
3140  p0    0:01  csh
3271  p0    0:00  sleep 60
3290  p0    0:00  ps
$
```

Note that there are three processes: the shell (**csh** in this example); **sleep**; and the **ps** command itself. After about 60 seconds, you should get the message:

```
I am awake now
```

Some systems will tell you when a background job has finished:

```
[1]   Done        (sleep 60; echo I am awake now)
$
```

Killing a Background Process

Sometimes it is necessary to stop a background process. This is done with the **kill** command. To see how this works, try the following command in background. Be sure to note the PID number:

    $(sleep 60; echo Stop this command) & RET
    3310

To kill the process, type *kill*, a space, and the PID number. Thus

    $kill 3271 RET

Some systems will tell you when a background job has been killed:

```
[1]   Terminated        (sleep 60; echo Stop this command)
$
```

Summary

These commands must be terminated by a RETURN.

sort *file*	sort contents of *file*
wc *file*	count lines, words, and characters in *file*
grep *pattern file*	search for *pattern* in *file*
sleep *n*	wait for *n* seconds
ps	check status of current processes
kill *m*	kill the background process number *m*

Exercises

(1)* **sort** has numerous options that control the way the sorting is carried out (reverse order, numerical order, ignoring blanks, etc.) Refer to the **man** entry for **sort**, and determine what each of the following commands is supposed to do:

```
sort -b

sort -d

sort -f

sort -n

sort -r

sort -nr
```

(2)* Refer to the **man** entry for **wc**, and determine what each of the following commands is supposed to do:

```
wc -l

wc -w

wc -c
```

(3)* Refer to the **man** entry for **grep**, and determine what each of the following commands is supposed to do:

```
grep -c pattern file

grep -i pattern file

grep -l pattern file

grep -n pattern file

grep -v pattern file
```

13. Startup Files

A *startup file* contains instructions that the shell executes when it begins running. Startup files can do many useful things for you, such as setting your terminal type, personalizing the prompt, and reminding you of important events.

Login Initialization Files

When you first log in, your login shell looks for its instructions in a startup file called the *login initialization file*. If you are using the **Bourne Shell (sh)** or **Korn Shell (ksh)**, this file will be called *.profile*; if you are using the **C Shell** as your login shell, this file will be called *.login*.

Note that these are hidden files—their names begin with a period (.)—meaning that they will not be listed by the simple **ls** command. Most hidden files are used to control the way the system works. For this reason, they are sometimes called *control files*. Some of the more common control files are listed below:

File	Contents
.cshrc	Commands to be run when a new shell starts up (**csh** only)
.forward	Addresses to which E-mail is forwarded
.kshrc	Commands to be run when a new shell starts up (**ksh** only)
.login	Commands to be run when you log in (**csh** only)
.logout	Commands to be run when you log out (**csh** only)
.mailrc	**mail** aliases (BSD UNIX only)
.newsrc	List of your network newsgroups and messages read
.plan	Information displayed by **finger** command
.profile	Commands to be run when you log in (**sh** & **ksh**)

Subshells and Startup Files

Most of the time you will use your login shell to interpret and execute the standard UNIX commands. Remember, however, that you can start a new shell—a subshell—just by typing the pathname of the file that contains the software for that shell. For example, you can start **sh** as a subshell simply by typing

$/bin/sh RET

Sometimes subshells are started for you automatically. If you run a program that you have written yourself, the login shell actually calls up a subshell to run the program. When the subshell is finished, it returns control to the login shell.

Whenever a new **ksh** or **csh** is started, either as a login shell or a subshell, it looks for instructions in a file called the *shell initialization file*. For the **ksh**, this file will be named *.kshrc*; for the **csh**, it will be named *.cshrc*. (The *rc* ending stands for "run command.")

Summary of Startup Files

Let's summarize what we have learned about startup files thus far:

- **sh** uses one startup file, named *.profile*. The shell executes the commands in this file only once, when you first log in.

- **ksh** uses two startup files. It executes the instructions in *.profile* and *.kshrc* when you first log in. After that, it executes *.kshrc* each time a **ksh** subshell is created.

- **csh** also uses two startup files. It executes the instructions in *.cshrc* and *.login* when you first log in. After that, it executes *.cshrc* each time a **csh** subshell is created. Finally, when you log out, **csh** executes instructions in file named *.logout*.

Variables

One of the most important uses for a startup file is to set the values of variables used by the shell. A *variable* is a named storage location that can hold a value. Three types of variables are commonly used by the shell:

- *Standard Shell Variables.* Also called *special shell variables, keyword variables, predefined shell variables,* or *environmental variables,* they are used to control the properties of the shell. Examples include TERM, HOME, and MAIL.

- *User-created Variables.* You can name your own variables and assign them values. These are also called *personal variables*.

- *Positional Parameters*. These are used in shell programs and are described in Chapters 16 and 17.

In this chapter we will discuss the standard shell variables and user-created variables.

Standard Shell Variables

The standard shell variables are often called *environmental shell variables* because they are used to tailor your computing environment to fit your needs.

Variable	Contents
HOME	the pathname of your home directory
PATH	the directories where the shell is to look for commands
SHELL	the pathname of the shell
TERM	the termcap code for your terminal
USER	your user name
PWD	the current working directory

Setting the Environmental Variables

Some of the standard shell variables (such as HOME and SHELL) are set automatically for you when you log in. Others (such as TERM) you must set yourself. This is usually done in your login initialization file.

If you are using either the **sh** or **ksh** as your login shell, you may put instructions in your *.profile* for setting up the values of the shell variables. For example, you could set the terminal type to be a vt100 by including this command line in your *.profile*:

```
TERM=vt100
```

Note that there are no spaces surrounding the equals sign. This command line tells the login shell that your terminal is a vt100, but you also need to get the information to any subshells that might be created as you are working. To do this, you must include the **export** command in your *.profile*:

```
export TERM
```

This will ensure that any subshells that are created are given the value of TERM. If for some reason you did not want the subshells to know what kind of terminal you are using, you could simply omit the **export** command.

The **csh** works a bit differently. You can set the terminal type and "export" it all at once by putting the **setenv** ("set environment") command in your *.login*:

```
setenv TERM vt100
```

The Values of the Variables

There are several ways to examine the value of a standard shell variable once it is set. If you are using **sh** or **ksh**, the **set** command without arguments will list all of the environmental variables such as TERM and PATH:

§set RET

If you are using **csh**, the **setenv** command without arguments will accomplish the same thing:

§setenv RET

You can also view the values of the individual variables one at a time with the **echo** command. For example, the following command line will display the current value of TERM:

§echo $TERM RET
vt100

Note the dollar sign ($) preceding TERM; this is a special character that tells **echo** you want to see the *contents* of the variable TERM, not just its name. If you omitted the dollar sign, this is what you would see:

```
$echo TERM RET
TERM
```

The Search Path

One of the important environmental variables is PATH, which tells the shell where to search for software to run commands. If you are using **sh** or **ksh**, your search path will be a list of pathnames, separated by colons (:). A typical search path might look something like this:

```
/bin:/usr/bin:/usr/yourlogin/bin
```

This tells the shell to look first in the */bin* directory. If it cannot find the right software in that directory, it is to search */usr/bin*, then */usr/yourlogin/bin*. The order of the directories is important. If different commands with the same name exist in more than one of the directories, the shell will execute the first one it finds and ignore the rest.

Placing a colon by itself at the beginning or end of the path, or two colons in a row within the path, tells the shell to search the current directory. Thus, each of the following search paths will cause the shell to look for software in the current directory:

```
:/bin:/usr/bin:/usr/yourlogin/bin

/bin:/usr/bin::/usr/yourlogin/bin

/bin:/usr/bin:/usr/yourlogin/bin:
```

The first string causes the current directory to be searched first. The second string causes the current directory to be searched after */bin* and */usr/bin*. The third sample string causes the current directory to be searched last.

The search path for the **csh** looks a bit different, but the idea is much the same. Instead of separating the directory pathnames by colons, the **csh** uses spaces. For example, the following search path tells the **csh** to search the */bin*, then */usr/bin*, then */usr/yourlogin/bin*:

```
( /bin /usr/bin /usr/yourlogin/bin )
```

To include the current directory in the search path, you would add *dot* (.) to the search string. Thus, to search the current directory first, the previous search string might be modified like this:

```
(. /bin /usr/bin /usr/yourlogin/bin )
```

To search the current directory last, you would place the *dot* at the end of the string:

```
( /bin /usr/bin /usr/yourlogin/bin . )
```

To search the current directory after */bin* and */usr/bin*, place *dot* this way:

```
( /bin /usr/bin . /usr/yourlogin/bin )
```

User-Defined Variables

In addition to the standard shell variables, you can define your own variables. This is done by giving the variable a name and a value. Suppose, for example, that you were frequently using a long directory name such as */usera/george/bin/stuff* and would prefer not to have to type it out each time. If you are using the **sh** or **ksh**, you could place the following line in your *.profile* to define a variable to hold the pathname:

```
stuff=/usera/george/bin/stuff
```

This creates a variable named `stuff`, and gives it the pathname as a value. This variable will be known only to the login shell; if you want it to be available to the subshells, you would have to "export" it:

```
export stuff
```

(If you are a **ksh** user, you could also make `stuff` available to the subshells by defining it in the *.kshrc* file.) Having defined the variable `stuff` and given it a value, you can use it to save keystrokes. For example, you could list the files in the directory */usera/george/bin/stuff* with the following command line:

```
§ls $stuff RET
```

The dollar sign in front of the variable name `stuff` is needed because you want to use the contents of the variable, not just its name.

csh handles user-defined variables a bit differently, but the idea is very much the same. To create the variable `stuff` you could use the **set** command in your *.login* file:

```
set stuff=/usera/george/bin/stuff
```

This would define `stuff` for the login shell, but the definition would not carry over to any subshells. If you want your subshells to be able to use this variable, you have two choices:

(1) Use the **setenv** command in your *.login* file:

```
setenv stuff /usera/george/bin/stuff
```

Remember, **setenv** sets the value of the variable and then "exports" it to all subshells.

(2) Use the **set** command in your *.cshrc* file:

```
set stuff=/usera/george/bin/stuff
```

Remember, any command in your *.cshrc* is run each time a new shell is created.

Traditionally, user-defined variable names are spelled in lowercase letters, to distinguish them from the standard shell variables.

The calendar Utility

Most UNIX systems offer the **calendar** utility, a kind of electronic datebook that you can use to remind yourself of important assignments, appointments, project deadlines, etc. (Do not confuse this with the **cal** utility, which displays a calendar on the screen.) If you want to use the **calendar**, you must include the following line in your startup file:

```
calendar
```

This command tells UNIX to search through a file named *calendar* for any lines that contain the current date, or the next day's date; it then displays those lines on the screen. (On weekends, it also displays Monday's messages.) Suppose you wanted to remember to call Adam Smith on April 12. You might put the following line in your *calendar* file:

```
Call Adam Smith April 12
```

When you log in on April 11, the computer will display the line

```
Call Adam Smith April 12
```

The same line will be displayed when you log in on April 12. Any of the following messages could be used instead:

```
Call Adam Smith on 4/12
April 12: call Adam Smith
Call Adam Smith on Apr 12
```

The date may appear anywhere on the line, and it may be spelled out (April 12), abbreviated (Apr 12), or written in numerals (4/12); however, you must put the month before the date. (Do not write 12 April, 12 Apr, or 12/4). If you include the year, it will be ignored; **calendar** always assumes the current year.

The history Mechanism (ksh & csh)

Another useful feature of the **Korn** and **C Shells** (but not the **Bourne Shell**) is the **history** mechanism, which keeps track of the most recent commands you have issued and gives you a quick way to repeat those commands. You can specify how many commands you want **history** to remember for you. Suppose, for example, that you have set up **history** to remember the last ten commands. (Most users set up the **history** mechanism to recall about 100 commands.) To remind yourself of ten most recent commands you have used, you would type

$history RET

This produces a numbered list of the commands you have used, including **history** itself:

```
 1     who | sort
 2     ls
 3     cal
 4     cd
 5     ls -l
 6     mkdir Stuff
 7     cd Stuff
 8     vi newstuff
 9     spell newstuff
10     history
```

You can repeat any of these commands. In **csh**, you simply type an exclamation mark (!) followed by the number to the left. Thus, to repeat command number 5, you would type

§ ! 5 RET
ls -l

In **ksh**, you would type *r* followed by the number of the command on the list:

§r 5 RET
ls -l

Aliases (ksh & csh)

The C and Korn Shells allow you to rename UNIX commands. A renamed command is called an *alias* of the original UNIX command and may be used to shorten long commands, or to protect you from accidentally deleting important information (such as with the **cp**, **mv**, or **rm** commands). Most users set up a list of aliases in their shell initialization file (*.kshrc* or *.cshrc*), so that the aliases are defined automatically each time a new shell is started.

The **alias** command is used to define aliases in **csh**. Placing the following line in the *.cshrc* file tells the shell to treat **m** as an alias for the **mail** command:

```
alias m mail
```

Once this is done, you could send mail to the user *bfranklin* with the command

§m bfranklin RET

ksh also uses **alias** to create aliases. The following line may be placed in the *.kshrc* file to create a **ksh** alias for the **mail** command:

```
alias m='mail'
```

Once this is done, you could send mail to the user *bfranklin* with the command

§m bfranklin RET

Exercises

(1)   Define: (a) startup file; (b) login initialization file; (c) subshell; (d) shell initialization file; (e) variable; (f) special shell variable; (g) environmental shell variable; (h) alias.

(2)   Suppose a **sh** user wanted to create a variable named myhome to hold the pathname of his or her home directory. (a) What command(s) should be put in the *.profile* so that myhome will be usable by the login shell only? (b) What command is needed if myhome is to be available to all subshells? (Hint: the shell variable HOME contains the pathname of the user's home directory.)

(3)   Suppose a **ksh** user wanted to create a variable named myhome to hold the pathname of his or her home directory. (a) What command(s) should be put in the *.profile* so that myhome will be usable by the login shell only? (b) What command(s) should be put in the *.profile* if myhome is to be available to all subshells? (c) What command(s) should be put in the file *.kshrc* to make myhome available to all subshells?

(4)   Suppose a **csh** user wanted to create a variable named myhome to hold the pathname of his or her home directory. (a) What command(s) should be put in the *.login* so that myhome will be usable by the login shell only? (b) What command(s) should be used in *.login* if myhome is to be available to all subshells? (c) What command(s) should be put in the file *.cshrc* to make myhome available to all subshells?

14. Tutorial: Creating sh or ksh Startup Files*

If your login shell is either the **Bourne Shell (sh)** or the **Korn Shell (ksh)**, your login initialization file will be named *.profile*. If you are a **ksh** user, you may also have a shell initialization file named *.kshrc*. In this chapter, you will learn how to make and modify such files.

Checking the Settings

Begin by checking the settings of the standard shell variables using the **set** command without arguments.

        $set RET

(Note the dollar sign prompt $; this is the default prompt for **sh** and **ksh**, and will be used in this chapter.) The shell will display a list of variables and their current settings. Some variables you might see include the following:

Variable	Contains
HOME	the pathname of your home directory
PATH	the directories where the shell is to look for commands
PS1	"prompt string 1"—the usual prompt string (default: $)
PS2	"prompt string 2"—the secondary prompt string (default: >)
SHELL	the pathname of the shell (*/bin/sh* for the **Bourne Shell**)
TERM	the termcap code for your terminal
MAIL	the pathname of the file where your mail is kept

You can examine the values of these variables one at a time with the **echo** command. Type this command, making sure to type a dollar sign before the variable name:

        $echo $PS2 RET

PS2 contains the secondary prompt. Its default value is

        >

If you omit the dollar sign in front of the variable name, the name of the variable, not its contents, will be displayed:

        $echo PS2 RET
        PS2

---

* If the **C Shell (csh)** is your login shell, you may wish to skip this chapter and go to the next one.

The Secondary Prompt

You might be wondering about the variable PS2: what exactly is the *secondary prompt*? The secondary prompt is a symbol that indicates that the shell is waiting for you to finish an incomplete command line. To see how this works, try the following command line, making sure not to type any closing quotes :

```
$echo "This is an RET
```

Because you did not provide the closing quotes, the shell assumes that there is more to come, and it displays the secondary prompt stored in PS2 (the default is a >):

```
>
```

Type in the rest of the command line, finishing it off with double quotes, and then a RETURN:

```
>incomplete command line." RET
```

The shell will echo back the entire message, then give you the usual prompt string:

```
This is an incomplete command line.
$
```

Comment Lines

Before you create or edit a *.profile*, you should know about comment lines. A *comment* is a line in a startup file (or a program) that is ignored by the shell when the file is executed. Comments are useful for reminding you (or someone else who might use your file) of the purpose of the file. In shell startup files, a comment begins with a pound sign (#). For example,

```
#This is a comment line
```

Creating a *.profile* File

The first step in creating a *.profile* file is to check to see whether you may already have one. Log in and set your terminal type, then type the **ls –a** ("list -all") command:

```
$ls  -a RET
.  ..
```

If you see a file named *.profile*, it means that your system administrator put one in your home directory. You should consult with your instructor or system administrator before editing this file. (If you are a **ksh** user, also note whether you already have a *.kshrc* file— more about this later.)

Note that two hidden directory names appeared when you used the **ls –a** command: *dot* and *dotdot*. Remember, *dot* stands for the current working directory itself, while *dotdot* refers to the *parent* of the working directory. Remember that every directory contains these hidden entries *dot* and *dotdot*, which are always listed by the **ls –a** command

A Login Message

Create a *.profile* file (or edit your existing file) to display a message on the screen each time you log in. Use the **echo** command to do this. First try out the **echo** command. Type

```
$echo "Your wish is my command, Oh Great One." RET
```

The shell should respond

```
Your wish is my command, Oh Great One.
```

Now use **vi** to open the *.profile* file:

```
$vi .profile RET
```

Insert the following line in *.profile*:

```
# This file was last modified on [today's date].
```

The first line begins with a #, making it a comment. This shows a typical use of a comment, which is to tell you when the file was last edited. Next, add the following line to the file:

```
echo "Your wish is my command, Oh Great One."
```

Write this into the file and quit the editor.

At this point, you *could* log out and log back in again to see if your *.profile* works. However, there is an easier way: use the "dot" command. Just type period, followed by a space and the name of the file:

```
$. .profile RET
```

This will cause the shell to execute the *.profile*. You should see the message

```
Your wish is my command, Oh Great One.
```

The shell will display this message each time you log in, unless you change it or delete it from your *.profile*.

Changing the Prompt Symbol

The default primary prompt symbol for **sh** or **ksh** is the dollar sign ($). You can change the prompt symbol by changing the values of the variable PS1. As an example, try changing the prompt symbol to the pound sign (#). Type the following line, making sure not to put spaces around the equals sign:

```
$PS1=# RET
```

This will change your shell prompt to the pound sign

```
#
```

Now try this line:

```
#PS1="Your Majesty? " RET
```

The quotes are needed here because the new prompt contains spaces. The prompt now should look like this:

```
Your Majesty?
```

You can also include shell variables in your prompt. Some people like to display the pathname of their home directory as part of their prompt. Remember, your home directory's pathname is stored by the shell in a variable named HOME. Try the following command (don't type "Your Majesty?"—it is the prompt):

```
Your Majesty? PS1="$HOME >" RET
```

The dollar sign placed in front of HOME tells the shell to put the *contents* of HOME in the prompt. Now your prompt should show the absolute pathname of your home directory, followed by an arrow (>). For example, if the absolute pathname of your home directory were */usr/you*, the prompt would now be

```
/usr/you >
```

(If you had left off the dollar sign, the word *HOME* would appear, instead of your home directory's pathname.) Let's put this prompt into your *.profile*. Use **vi** to open *.profile*, and add the following lines to the file:

```
PS1= "$HOME >"
export PS1
```

Write and quit, and use the "dot" command to run *.profile*:

```
/usr/you >. .profile RET
```

Your prompt should now consist of your home directory's pathname, followed by an arrow. Thus, if your home directory were */usr/you*, you would see your login message, then the prompt

```
/usr/you >
```

Setting the Terminal Type

Having to set your terminal each time you log in is a nuisance if you use the same kind of terminal all of the time. If your system does not ask for your terminal each time you log in, you can set the terminal in your *.profile* file. Use the **vi** editor to add the following lines in your *.profile* file, substituting your terminal's termcap code for *code*:

```
TERM=code
export TERM
echo "Remember to set terminal type (default: code)"
```

Write and quit the editor, then try the "dot" command:

```
/usr/you > . .profile RET
```

Your login message should appear, then the reminder

```
Remember to set terminal type (default: code)
```

Making a *calendar* File

If you want to use the **calendar** utility to remind yourself of upcoming events, open your *.profile* with the **vi** editor and add the following line:

```
calendar
```

Write this into the file and quit **vi**. Next you have to create a file *calendar*, which must be in your home directory. Use the **vi** editor to create the new file. After the prompt (/usr/you >) type

```
/usr/you >vi calendar RET
```

Be careful to use this exact spelling of *calendar*, in lowercase letters; otherwise, the shell won't recognize the file name.

Put a message into the calendar file using today's date:

```
This is a test for [today's date]
```

Write this into the *calendar* file, quit the editor, and use the "dot" command on *.profile*:

```
/usr/you >. .profile RET
```

You should see your login message, the reminder to set your terminal, and the *calendar* message:

```
Your wish is my command, Oh Great One.
Remember to set terminal type (default: code)
This is a test for [today's date]
```

Creating a .kshrc (ksh only)

If you are a **ksh** user, you may create a shell initialization file named *.kshrc*. This file is typically used for setting up command aliases and the **history** mechanism. Before doing this, however, you need to put the following lines in your *.profile*:

```
ENV=$HOME/.kshrc
export ENV
```

This tells **ksh** that it should look for *.kshrc* in your home directory. If the ENV variable is not set, **ksh** will not execute *.kshrc*.

Next, use the **vi** editor to open up *.kshrc*. Start by putting in a comment line, giving today's date:

```
# This file was last modified on [today's date]
```

Add the following line to the file to create an alias for the **history** command:

```
alias -x h=history
```

The **-x** option tells **alias** to export the alias to all subshells. To see how the alias works, write to the file and quit the editor. Then use the "dot" command to run the *.kshrc* file:

```
/usr/you >..kshrc RET
```

Now type *h* followed by RETURN to run the **history** command:

```
/usr/you >h RET
```

If everything is working properly, you should see a numbered list of the most recently executed commands—something like this:

```
1     set
2     echo $PS2
3     echo PS2
4     echo "This is an incomplete command line."
5     ls -a
6     echo "Your wish is my command, Oh Great One."
7     vi .profile
8     . .profile
9     PS1=#
10    PS1="Your Majesty? "
11    PS1="$HOME >"
12    vi .profile
13    . .profile
14    vi .profile
15    . .profile
16    vi .profile
17    vi .calendar
18    . .kshrc
19    h
```

Using the history Mechanism

The **history** mechanism permits you to repeat the most recent command on the history list simply by typing an *r*. Try it:

```
/usr/you >r RET
```

If you have been following the text carefully, the most recent command is the **history** command itself. You should see a listing very similar to this:

```
1     set
2     echo $PS2
3     echo PS2
4     echo "This is an incomplete command line."
5     ls -a
6     echo "Your wish is my command, Oh Great One."
7     vi .profile
8     . .profile
9     PS1=#
10    PS1="Your Majesty? "
11    PS1="$HOME >"
12    vi .profile
13    . .profile
14    vi .profile
15    . .profile
16    vi .profile
17    vi .calendar
18    . .kshrc
19    h
20    h
```

You can repeat a command by its number on the list. For example,

```
/usr/you >r 6 RET
echo "Your wish is my command, Oh Great One."
Your wish is my command, Oh Great One.
```

You can also repeat a command by giving just the first letter(s) of the command line:

```
/usr/you >r s RET
set
```

The most recent command beginning with *s* is the **set** command; it should list the values of the environmental variables.

Most users set up their **history** mechanism to remember about 100 commands. To do this yourself, open your *.kshrc* file and insert this line:

```
HISTSIZE=100
```

If you neglect to set the HISTSIZE variable, **ksh** will remember the most recent 128 commands by default.

Exercises

(1)* The **date** command prints the date and current time. Add the following line to your *.profile*, making sure to use backquotes around **date**:

```
echo "The date and time are `date`."
```

Exit the editor and run the *.profile* using the "dot" command. What happens?

(2)* The backquotes were needed in the previous exercise to tell the shell that **date** was to be interpreted as a command, not as a word. Open up your *.profile* and remove the backquotes from **date**:

```
echo "The date and time are date"
```

Exit the editor and run the *.profile* using the "dot" command. What happens? (Now open up the file and replace the backquotes.)

(3)* What is your search path?

(4)* What is the complete pathname for your shell?

(5)* The **rm** command is dangerous because it does not stop you from accidentally removing a file. Some UNIX systems offer a −**i** (for "interactive") option on **rm**. With this option, **rm** will ask you whether you wish to remove the file. Use the **man** command to see if the −**i** option is available to you. If it is, try using this command on a file that you do not need.

(6)* Suppose the following lines are placed in your *.kshrc* file:

```
alias -x m=more
alias -x f=finger
alias -x cp -i
alias -x mv -i
```

Explain what each alias would do.

15. Tutorial: Using csh Special Files*

If your login shell is the **C Shell** (**csh**), your login initialization file will be named *.login*, and your shell initialization file will be named *.cshrc*. You may also have a *.logout* file containing commands that **csh** executes when you log out. In this chapter, you will learn how to make and modify these files.

Checking the Environmental Variables

You can check the settings of the environmental variables using the **setenv** command without any arguments:

```
%setenv RET
```

(Note the percent sign prompt %; this is the default prompt for **csh**, and will be used in this chapter.)The shell will display a list of the environmental variables and their current settings. Some variables you might see include the following:

Variable	Contains
HOME	the pathname of your home directory
PATH	the directories where the shell is to look for commands
SHELL	the pathname of the shell (*/bin/csh* for the **C Shell**)
TERM	the termcap code for your terminal
PWD	the current working directory

You can examine the values of these variables one at a time with the **echo** command. Type this command, making sure to type a dollar sign before the variable name:

```
%echo $SHELL RET
```

This will display the absolute pathname of **csh**:

```
/bin/csh
```

If you omit the dollar sign in front of the variable name, the name of the variable, not its contents, will be displayed:

```
%echo SHELL RET
SHELL
```

---

* If you do not intend to use the **C Shell**, you can skip this chapter.

Checking the Special csh Variables

csh uses the same environmental variables as **sh** and **ksh**, but adds some special shell variables of its own. Check the settings of these special **csh** variables using the **set** command without arguments:

```
%set RET
```

The shell will display a list of variables and their current settings. For example,

Variable	Contains
cwd	the pathname of the current working directory
history	the number of commands remembered by the **history** mechanism
home	the pathname of your home directory
path	the directories where the shell is to look for commands
prompt	the current prompt symbol (default is %)
shell	the pathname of the shell (*/bin/csh*)
term	the termcap code for your terminal
user	your login name

These are special shell variables used only by **csh**, not by **sh** or **ksh**. Note that the **csh** special variables are written in lowercase letters. Their value is set using the **set** command. Set the value of the history variable:

```
%set history=100 RET
```

This tells **history** to retain the 100 most recent commands.

Some of the special **csh** variables have a special relationship with their uppercase counterparts. If you run the **set** command to change the value of term, for instance, the value of TERM is automatically changed to match.

Comment Lines

Before you create or edit a *.login*, you should know about comment lines. A *comment* is a line in a startup file (or a program) that is ignored by the shell when the file is executed. Comments are useful for reminding you (or someone else who might use your file) of the purpose of the file. In shell startup files, a comment begins with a pound sign (#). For example,

```
#This is a comment line
```

Do You Have a *.login*, *.cshrc*, or *.logout*?

The first step is to check to see whether you may already have a *.login*, *.cshrc*, or *.logout*. Log in and set your terminal type, then type the **ls –a** ("list –all") command:

```
%ls -a RET
```

If you see a *.login* or *.cshrc* file, it means that your system administrator put one in your home directory. You should consult with the system administrator before editing these files.

Note that the two hidden directories *dot* and *dotdot* were listed by the **ls –a** command. Remember, *dot* stands for the current working directory itself, while *dotdot* refers to the *parent* of the working directory. Every directory contains these hidden entries *dot* and *dotdot*.

A Login Message

Create a *.login* file (or edit your existing file) to display a message on the screen each time you log in. Use the **echo** command to do this. First try out the **echo** command. Type

```
%echo "Your wish is my command, Oh Great One." RET
```

The shell should respond

```
Your wish is my command, Oh Great One.
```

Now use **vi** to open the *.login* file:

```
%vi .login RET
```

Insert the following line in *.login*:

```
# This file was last modified on [today's date].
```

The first line begins with a #, making it a comment. This shows a typical use of a comment, which is to tell you when the file was last edited. Next, add the following line to the file:

```
echo "Your wish is my command, Oh Great One."
```

Write this into the file and quit the editor.

At this point, you *could* log out and log back in again to see how your *.login* file works. However, there is an easier way. The **source** command causes the shell to execute the file:

```
%source .login
```

You should see

```
Your wish is my command, Oh Great One.
```

The shell will display this message each time you log in, unless you change it or delete it from your *.login* file.

Changing the Prompt Symbol

The default prompt symbol for the **C Shell** is the percent sign (%). You can change the prompt symbol by changing the value of prompt using the **set** command. Try this line:

```
%set prompt=#RET
```

This will change your shell prompt to the pound sign

```
#
```

Now try this line:

```
#set prompt="Your Majesty? "RET
```

The quotes are needed here because the new prompt contains spaces. The prompt now should look like this:

```
Your Majesty?
```

You can also include shell variables in your prompt. Some people, for example, like to display the pathname of their home directory as part of their prompt. Remember, your home directory's pathname is stored by the shell in a variable named "home" (or HOME). Try the following command (don't type "Your Majesty?"—it is the prompt):

```
Your Majesty?set prompt="$home >"RET
```

The dollar sign placed in front of home tells the shell to put the *contents* of home in the prompt. Now your prompt should show the absolute pathname of your home directory, followed by an arrow (>). For example, if the absolute pathname of your home directory were */usr/you*, the prompt would now be

```
/usr/you >
```

(If you had left off the dollar sign, the word *home* would appear, instead of your home directory's pathname.) Let's put this prompt into your *.login*. Use **vi** to open *.login*, and add the following line to the file:

```
set prompt="$home >"
```

Write and quit, and issue the **source** command:

```
source .loginRET
```

Your prompt should now consist of your home directory's pathname, followed by an arrow. Thus, if your home directory were */usr/you*, you would see

```
/usr/you >
```

Setting the Terminal Type

Having to set your terminal each time you log in is a nuisance if you use the same kind of terminal all of the time. If your system does not ask for your terminal each time you log in, you can set the terminal in your *.login* file. Use the **vi** editor to add the following lines in your *.login* file, substituting your terminal's termcap code for *code*:

```
set term=code
echo "Remember to set terminal type (default: code)"
```

Write and quit the editor, then try the source command:

```
/usr/you >source .login RET
```

You should see the login message and the terminal message:

```
Your wish is my command, Oh Great One.
Remember to set terminal type (default: code)
```

Creating a *calendar* File

If you want to use the **calendar** utility to remind yourself of upcoming events, you must include the following line in your startup file:

```
calendar
```

This command tells UNIX to search through a file named **calendar** for any lines that contain the current date, or the next day's date; it then displays those lines on the screen. (On weekends, it displays Monday's messages.) Obviously, then, you have to create a file **calendar**. This file must be in your home directory. Use the **vi** editor to create the new file. After the prompt (/usr/you >) type

```
/usr/you >vi calendar RET
```

Be careful to use this exact spelling of *calendar*, in lowercase letters; otherwise, the shell won't recognize the file name.

Now you can put something into the **calendar** file. Open **calendar** with **vi** and insert the following line, using today's date in the appropriate place:

```
This is a test for [today's date]
```

The date may appear anywhere on the line, and it may be spelled out (April 12), abbreviated (Apr 12), or written in numerals (4/12); however, you must put the month before the date. (Do not write 12 April, 12 Apr, or 12/4). If you include the year, it will be ignored; **calendar** always assumes the current year.

Write this into the **calendar** file, quit the editor, and use the **source** command on *.login*:

```
/usr/you >source .login RET
```

You should see your login message, the reminder to set your terminal, and the *calendar* message:

```
Your wish is my command, Oh Great One.
Remember to set terminal type (default: code)
This is a test for [today's date]
```

Creating a .cshrc

The *.cshrc* file is typically used for setting up command aliases and the **history** mechanism. Use the **vi** editor to open up *.cshrc*. Start by putting in a comment line giving today's date:

```
# This file was last modified on [today's date]
```

Next add the following line to the file to create an alias for the **history** command:

```
alias h history
```

Write this to the file and quit the editor. Then use the **source** command on the *.cshrc* file:

```
/usr/you >source .cshrc RET
```

To see how the alias works, type *h* followed by RETURN to run the **history** command:

```
/usr/you >h RET
```

If everything is working properly, you should see a numbered list of the most recently executed commands—something like this:

```
1      set history=100
2      ls -a
3      echo "Your wish is my command, Oh Great One."
4      vi .login
5      source .login
6      set prompt=#
7      set prompt="Your Majesty? "
8      set prompt"$home >"
9      vi .login
10     source .login
11     vi .login
12     source .login
13     vi .login
14     vi calendar
15     source .login
16     vi .cshrc
17     source .cshrc
18     h
```

Using the history Mechanism

The **history** mechanism permits you to repeat the most recent command simply by typing two exclamation points (!!). Try it:

```
/usr/you >!! RET
```

If you have been following the text carefully, the most recent command is the **history** command itself. You should see something like this:

```
1       set history=100
2       ls -a
3       echo "Your wish is my command, Oh Great One."
4       vi .login
5       source .login
6       set prompt=#
7       set prompt="Your Majesty? "
8       set prompt"$home >"
9       vi .login
10      source .login
11      vi .login
12      source .login
13      vi .login
14      vi calendar
15      source .login
16      vi .cshrc
17      source .cshrc
18      h
19      h
```

You can repeat a command by its number on the list. For example,

```
/usr/you >!3 RET
echo "Your wish is my command, Oh Great One."
Your wish is my command, Oh Great One.
```

You can also repeat a command by giving just the first letter(s) of the command line:

```
/usr/you >!s RET
source .cshrc
```

The most recent command line beginning with *s* runs the **source** command.

Most users set up the **history** mechanism to remember about 100 commands. You can do this by inserting the following line in your *.cshrc* file:

```
set history=100
```

If you neglect to do this, you will have to set history each time you log in, or else **csh** will not remember any commands.

Exercises

(1)* The **date** command prints the date and current time. Add the following line to your *.login*, making sure to use backwards single quotes around **date**:

```
echo "The date and time are `date`"
```

Exit the editor and run the *.login* using the **source** command. What happens?

(2)* The backquotes were needed in the previous exercise to tell the shell that **date** was to be interpreted as a command, not as a word. Open up your **.login** and remove the backquotes from **date**:

```
echo "The date and time are date"
```

Exit the editor and run the *.login* using the **source** command. What happens? (Be sure to replace the backquotes on **date**.)

(3)* What is your search path?

(4)* What is the complete pathname for your shell?

(5)* The **rm** command is dangerous because it does not stop you from accidentally removing a file. Some UNIX systems offer a –**i** (for "interactive") option on **rm**. With this option, **rm** will ask you whether you wish to remove the file. Use the **man** command to see if the –**i** option is available to you. If it is, try using this command on a file that you do not need.

(6)* Suppose the following lines are placed in your *.cshrc* file:

```
alias m more
alias f finger
alias cp cp -i
alias mv mv -i
alias rm rm -i
```

Explain what each alias would do.

Part VI
SHELL SCRIPTS

16. Shell Scripts

Until now, you have been giving commands to the UNIX shell by typing them on the keyboard. When used this way, the shell is said to be a *command interpreter*. The shell can also be used as a high-level programming language. Instead of entering commands one at a time in response to the shell prompt, you can put a number of commands in a file, to be executed all at once by the shell. A program consisting of shell commands is called a *shell script*. This chapter will introduce you to shell scripts for the **Bourne Shell**.

A Simple Shell Script

Suppose you were to make up a file named *commands* containing the following lines:

```
# A simple shell script
cal
date
who
```

The first line in this file begins with a # symbol, which indicates a comment line. Anything following the # is ignored by the shell. The remaining three lines are shell commands: the first produces a calendar for the current month, the second gives the current date and time, and the third lists the users currently logged onto the computer.

One way to get the **Bourne Shell** (**sh**) to run these commands is to type

$sh < commands RET

The redirection operator (<) tells the shell to take its commands from the file *commands* instead of from the standard input. It turns out, however, that the redirection symbol is not really needed in this case. Thus, you can also run the commands in the *commands* file by typing

$sh commands RET

Is there any way to set up the file *commands* so that you can run it without explicitly invoking the shell? In other words, can you run *commands* without first typing **sh**, **csh**, or **ksh**? The answer is yes, but you first have to make the file *executable*. The **chmod** command is used to change *commands* to an executable file:

$chmod u+x commands RET

The argument u+x tells **chmod** that you want to add (+) permission for the user (u) to execute (x) the shell script in the file.* Now all you need do is type the file name

$commands RET

and the shell will run the commands in the file.

---

* The **chmod** command is described in Appendix B.

Subshells

When you tell the shell to run a script such as the ***commands*** file, your login shell actually calls up another shell to run the script. (Remember, the shell is just another program, and UNIX can run more than one program at a time.) The new shell process is called a *subshell* or *child* of the original shell. The parent shell waits for its child to finish, then takes over and gives you a prompt.

§

Incidentally, a subshell can be different from its parent shell. For example, you can have **csh** or **ksh** as your login shell, but use **sh** to run your shell scripts. Many users in fact do this. When it comes time to run a script, the **csh** or **ksh** simply calls up the **sh** to do the job.

We will always use **sh** for running shell scripts. To make sure that **sh** is used, we will include the following line at the top of each shell script file:

```
#!/bin/sh
```

Thus, our **commands** file would look something like this:

```
#!/bin/sh
# A simple shell script
cal
date
who
```

The Shell as a Programming Language

The sample script **commands** is almost trivial—it does nothing more than execute three simple commands that you could just as easily type into the standard input. The shell can actually do much more. It is, in fact, a sophisticated programming language, with many of the same features found in other programming languages, including

- Variables
- Input/Output Functions
- Arithmetic Operations
- Conditional Expressions
- Selection Structures
- Iteration Structures

We will discuss each of these in order.

Variables

There are three types of variables commonly used in shell scripts:

- *Standard Shell Variables.* Sometimes called *special shell variables, keyword variables, predefined shell variables,* or *environmental variables,* they are used to tailor the operating environment to suit your needs. Examples include TERM, HOME, and MAIL.

- *User-created Variables.* You can name your own variables and assign them values.

- *Positional Parameters.* These are used by the shell to store the values of command arguments.

Of these, the special shell variables and user-created variables have been introduced already. The positional parameters, however, are new, and since they are very useful in shell programming, we will examine them in some detail now.

The *positional parameters* are also called *read-only variables,* or *automatic variables,* because the shell sets them for you automatically. They "capture" the values of the command-line arguments that are to be used by a shell script. The positional parameters are are numbered 0, 1, 2, 3, ... 9. To illustrate their use, consider the following shell script, and assume that it is contained in an executable file named *echo.args*:

```
#!/bin/sh
# Illustrate the use of positional parameters
echo $0 $1 $2 $3 $4 $5 $6 $7 $8 $9
```

Suppose you run the script by typing the command line

```
$echo.args We like UNIX. RET
```

The shell stores the name of the command ("echo.args") in the parameter $0; it puts the argument "We" in the parameter $1; it puts "like" in the parameter $2, and "UNIX." in parameter $3. Since that takes care of all the arguments, the rest of the parameters are left empty. Then the script echoes them back:

```
echo.args We like UNIX.
```

What if the user types in more than nine arguments? The positional parameter $* contains all of the arguments $1, $2, $3, ... $9, and any arguments beyond these nine. Thus, we can rewrite *echo.args* to handle any number of arguments:

```
#!/bin/sh
# Illustrate the use of positional parameters
echo $*
```

The parameter $# contains the number of arguments that the user typed. We can modify the script *echo.args* once again to use this parameter:

```
#!/bin/sh
# Illustrate the use of positional parameters
echo You typed $# arguments: $*
```

Suppose we were then to type the command line

$echo.args To be or not to be [RET]

The computer would respond with

```
You typed 6 arguments: To be or not to be
```

Input Using the read Statement

The positional parameters are useful for capturing command-line arguments but they have a limitation: once the script begins running, the positional parameters cannot be used for obtaining more input from the standard input. For this you have to use the **read** statement. Let's modify the previous program to make use of **read**:

```
#!/bin/sh
# Illustrate the use of positional parameters
# user-defined variables and the read command.
echo 'What is your name?'
read name
echo "Well, $name, you typed $# arguments:"
echo "$*"
```

In this script, name is a user-defined variable. The **read** command reads the user's response and stores it in name. With this modification, the script *echo.args* works something like this:

$echo.args To be or not to be [RET]

The computer would respond with the prompt:

```
What is your name?
```

Suppose you were to type

Rumpelstiltskin[RET]

The computer would respond with

```
Well, Rumpelstiltskin, you typed 6 arguments:
To be or not to be
```

The set Command

The positional parameters are sometimes called *read-only variables*, because the shell sets their values for you when you type arguments to the script. However, you can also set their values using the **set** command. To illustrate this, consider the following shell script, which we will assume is in the file *setdate*:

```
#!/bin/sh
# Demonstrate the set command
set `date`
echo "Time: $4 $5"
echo "Day: $1"
echo "Date: $3 $2 $6
```

Assuming that *setdate* has been made executable with the **chmod** command, we can run the script by typing the command

$setdate RET

The output will look something like this:

```
Time: 10:56:08
Day: Fri
Date: 13 Aug 1999
```

What happened? Consider the command line

```
set `date`
```

The backquotes runs the **date** command, which produces output something like this:

```
Fri Aug 13 10:56:08 EST 1999
```

This does not appear on the screen. Instead, the **set** command catches the output and stores it in the positional parameters $1–$6:

Parameter	Contains
$1	Fri
$2	Aug
$3	13
$4	10:56:08
$5	EST
$6	1999

Arithmetic Operations Using the expr Utility

The shell is not intended for numerical work—if you have to do a lot of calculations, you should consider C, FORTRAN, or Pascal. Nevertheless, the **expr** utility may be used to perform simple arithmetic operations on integers. (**expr** is not a shell command, but rather a separate UNIX utility; however, it is most often used in shell scripts.) To use it in a shell script, you simply surround the expression with back quotes. For example, let's write a simple script called **sum** that adds two numbers typed as arguments:

```
#!/bin/sh
# Add two numbers
sum=`expr $1 + $2`
echo $sum
```

Here we defined a variable sum to hold the result of the operation. (Note the spaces around the plus sign, but not around the equals sign.) To run this script, we might type the following line:

```
$sum 4 3 RET
```

The first argument (4) is stored in $1, and the second (3) is stored in $2. The **expr** utility then adds these quantities and stores the result in sum. Finally, the contents of sum are echoed on the screen:

```
7
$
```

The **expr** command only works on integers (i.e., whole numbers). It can perform the following operations:

+	addition
−	subtraction
*	multiplication
/	division
%	remainder

Control Structures

Normally, the shell processes the commands in a script sequentially, one after another in the order they are written in the file. Often, however, you will want to change the way that commands are processed. You may want to choose to run one command or another, depending on the circumstances; or you may want to run a command more than once.

To alter the normal sequential execution of commands, the shell offers a variety of *control structures*. There are two types of *selection structures*, which allow a choice between alternative commands:

if/then/elif/else/fi

case

There are three types of *repetition* or *iteration structures* for carrying out commands more than once:

for

while

until

The if Statement and test Command

The **if** statement lets you choose whether to run a particular command (or group of commands), depending on some condition. The simplest version of this structure has the general form

if *conditional expression*
then
    command(s)
fi

When the shell encounters a structure such as this, it first checks to see whether the *conditional expression* is true. If so, the shell runs any commands that it finds between the **then** and the **fi** (which is just **if** spelled backwards). If the *conditional expression* is not true, the shell skips the commands between **then** and **fi**. Here is an example of a shell script that uses a simple **if** statement:

```
#!/bin/sh
set `date`
if test $1 = Fri
then
        echo "Thank goodness it's Friday!"
fi
```

Here we have used the **test** command in our conditional expression. The expression

```
test $1 = Fri
```

checks to see if the parameter $1 contains Fri; if it does, the **test** command reports that the condition is true, and the message is printed.

The **test** command can carry out a variety of different tests; some of the arguments that it takes are listed below:

Argument	Test is true if
-d *file*	*file* is a directory
-f *file*	*file* is an ordinary file
-r *file*	*file* is readable
-s *file*	*file* size is greater than zero
-w *file*	*file* is writable
-x *file*	*file* is executable
n1 -eq *n2*	integer *n1* equals integer *n2*
n1 -ge *n2*	integer *n1* greater than or equal to integer *n2*
n1 -gt *n2*	integer *n1* greater than integer *n2*
n1 -le *n2*	integer *n1* less than or equal to integer *n2*
n1 -ne *n2*	integer *n1* not equal to integer *n2*
n1 -lt *n2*	integer *n1* less than integer *n2*
s1 = *s2*	string *s1* equals string *s2*
s1 != *s2*	string *s1* not equal to string *s2*

The elif and else Statements

We can make the selection structures much more elaborate by combining the **if** with the **elif** ("else if") and **else** statements. Here is a simple example:

```
#!/bin/sh
set `date`
if test $1 = Fri
then
      echo "Thank goodness it's Friday!"
elif test $1 = Sat  || test $1 = Sun
then
      echo "You should not be here working."
      echo "Log off and go home."
else
      echo "It is not yet the weekend."
      echo "Get to work!"
fi
```

Here, the first conditional expression is tested to see if the day is a Friday. If it is, the message "Thank goodness it's Friday!" is printed, and the shell script is finished. If not, the second conditional expression is tested. Note that we have used the OR operator (| |) in this expression to test whether the day is a Saturday or Sunday, in which case the message will be printed, and the script is finished. Otherwise, the third message is printed.

We could make even more elaborate selection structures by including more **elif** clauses. The important thing to note about such structures is that only one of the alternatives may be chosen; as soon as one is, the remaining choices are skipped.

The case Statement

The shell provides another selection structure that may run faster than the **if** statement on some UNIX systems. This is the **case** statement, and it has the following general form:

> **case** *word* **in**
> *pattern1*) *command(s)* ;;
> *pattern2*) *command(s)* ;;
> ...
> **esac**

The **case** statement compares *word* with *pattern1*; if they match, the shell runs the commands on the first line. Otherwise, the shell checks the remaining patterns, one by one, until it finds one that matches the *word*; it then runs the command(s) on that line.

Let's write a simple shell script using the **case** statement:

```
#!/bin/sh
set `date`
case $1 in
Fri) echo "Thank goodness it's Friday!";;
Sat | Sun) echo "You should not be here working";
          echo "Log off and go home!";;
*)   echo "It is not yet the weekend.";
     echo "Get to work!";;
esac
```

There are a few points to note about this structure. First, commands are separated by semicolons (;), and the end of a group of commands is indicated by two semicolons (; ;). The OR symbol used in case statements is a single vertical line (|), not the double vertical lines (| |) used in the **if** statement. The last pattern (*) is the default case, which is selected if none of the other patterns are matched.

for Loops

Sometimes we want to run a command (or group of commands) over and over. This is called *iteration, repetition,* or *looping.* The most commonly used shell iteration structure is the **for** loop, which has the general form

> **for** *variable* **in** *list*
> **do**
>   *command(s)*
> **done**

Here is a simple application of the **for** loop:

```
#!/bin/sh
#
for name in $*
do
     finger $name
done
```

Each time through the **for** loop, the user-defined variable name takes on the value of the next arguments in the list $*. This is then used as the argument to the **finger** command. Assuming this script is contained in the executable file *fingerall*, it would be run by typing the name of the file, followed by the login names you wish to finger:

```
$fingerall johnp maryl frederick RET
```

while Loops

The general form of the **while** loop is

> **while** *condition*
> **do**
> > *command(s)*
> **done**

As long as the *condition* is true, the commands between the **do** and the **done** are executed. Here is an example of a shell script that uses the **expr** utility with the **while** loop to print a message ten times:

```
#!/bin/sh
# Print a message ten times
count=10
while `expr $count`
do
      echo "   "
      `expr $count - 1`
done
```

until Loop

Another kind of iteration structure is the **until** loop. It has the general form

> **until** *condition*
> **do**
> > *command(s)*
> **done**

This loop continues to execute the *command(s)* between the **do** and **done** until the *condition* is true. We can rewrite the previous script using an **until** instead of the **while** loop:

```
#!/bin/sh
# Print a message ten times
count=10
until $count = 0
do
      echo "     "
      `expr $count - 1`
done
```

Exercises

1. Define: (a) shell script; (b) comment; (c) subshell; (d) positional parameter; (e) control structure; (f) selection structure; (g) repetition structures; (h) iteration; (i) loop.

2.* Try writing and running each of the sample programs shown in this chapter.

17. Tutorial: Creating Shell Scripts

In this chapter we consider a number of shell scripts that make use of the programming features presented in the previous chapter. Before presenting the actual code for each script, we will follow the general outline of the **man** pages and present the name of the script, a brief synopsis of how the script is used, and a description of how the script works.

Making a File Executable: *chex*

If you are planning to write a lot of shell scripts, you will find it convenient to have a script that will change files to be executable. Let's write such a script, and call it *chex*.

> NAME
> > *chex*—change a file to be executable
>
> SYNOPSIS
> > `chex filename`
>
> DESCRIPTION
> > This is the pseudocode for *chex* :
> >
> > > Select **sh**
> > > Use **chmod a+x** on the filename given as an argument (in $1)
> > > Tell the user that the file is now executable
> > > Use **ls –l** to show the modes on the file

Use the **vi** editor to open a file named *chex*, and put the following lines in the file:

```
#!/bin/sh
# Make a file executable
chmod a+x $1
echo $1 is now executable:
ls -l $1
```

Once you have finished, write and quit the file. Since *chex* is not yet executable, you will first need to make *chex* executable itself. One way to do this is to tell the shell to run *chex* on itself. Try this command line:

```
%sh chex chex RET
```

This tells the shell to run *chex*, taking *chex* itself as the argument. The result is that *chex* makes itself executable. The output from this command will look something like this:

```
chex is now executable:
-rwxrwx--x      1    yourlogin   59    Date time chex
```

Now that *chex* is executable, you can use it to change the other files' protections to executable.

Labeling the Output from wc: *mywc*

The **wc** ("word count") filter counts the words, lines, and characters in a file. For example, try running **wc** on the *chex* file you have just created:

```
$wc chex RET
4    12    59    chex
$
```

The output tells us that there are 4 lines, 12 words, and 59 characters in the file *chex*. This can be very useful information, but it would be a bit more convenient to use if the output were labeled.

> NAME
> > *mywc*—labeled word count
>
> SYNOPSIS
> > mywc *filename*
>
> DESCRIPTION
> > This is the pseudocode for *mywc*:
> >
> > > Select **sh**
> > > Run **wc** on $1, and capture the output with the **set** command
> > > Print the filename ($4)
> > > Print the number of lines ($1)
> > > Print the number of words ($2)
> > > Print the number of characters ($3)

Create a file named *mywc* containing the following shell script:

```
#!/bin/sh
# Label the output from wc
set `wc $1`
echo "File: $4"
echo "Lines: $1"
echo "Words: $2"
echo "Characters: $3"
```

Write and quit, then use *chex* to make the new script executable:

```
$chex mywc RET
mywc is now executable:
-rwxrwx--x    1   yourlogin   59   Date time chex
```

Now try *mywc* on the file *chex*:

```
$mywc chex RET
File: chex
Lines: 4
Words: 12
Characters: 59
```

Removing Files Safely: *del*

The **rm** command can be very dangerous because it allows you to remove a file, but does not give you a way of getting back a file you may have removed accidentally. Some UNIX systems allow you to use **rm** with the **–i** (interactive) option; it will ask you if you are sure you want to remove the file in question. Let's create a similar command for removing files that will ask you if you want to remove the file *and* tell what has been done with the file.

NAME
> *del*—delete a file interactively

SYNOPSIS
> del *filename*

DESCRIPTION
> This is the pseudocode for *del*:

> > Select **sh**
> > Get the filename from the command line ($1)
> > If there is no file with that name
> > > print an error message
> > Otherwise
> > > Ask if the user really wants to delete the file
> > > Read the user's choice (y/n)
> > > If the choice is yes (y)
> > > > remove the file & print a message
> > > otherwise
> > > > print a message

Open a file named *del*, and enter the following lines:

```
#!/bin/sh
# Delete a file interactively
filename=$1
if test ! -f $filename
then
     echo "There is no file \"$filename\"."
else
     echo "Do you want to delete \"$filename\"?"
     read choice
     if  test  $choice = y
     then
          rm $filename
          echo "\"$filename\" deleted."
     else
          echo "\"$filename\" not deleted."
     fi
fi
```

Now use **chex** to make the *del* file executable:

```
$chex del RET
del is now executable:
-rwxrw----      1    yourlogin   347   Date time del
```

A Daily Reminder System: *tickle*

We have already seen how you can use the **calendar** utility to remind yourself of important events. One limitation of **calendar** is that you have to enter each event individually, along with its date. This can be a problem for routine events that happen every day or every week. For reminding yourself of such events, the following *tickle* script can be very useful. It uses the **date** command to check the day of the week, then prints out an appropriate message.

> NAME
> > *tickle*—a daily reminder service
>
> SYNOPSIS
> > tickle
>
> DESCRIPTION
> > This is the pseudocode for *tickle*:
> >
> > > Select **sh**
> > > Use **set** to capture the output from **date**
> > > Print a message
> > > Check the day ($1) and print an appropriate message

Open up a file named *tickle*, and enter the following script:

```
#!/bin/sh
# A weekly reminder service
set `date`
echo "Remember for today:"
case $1 in
    Mon) echo "Plan the week.";;
    Tue) echo "Take clothes to the cleaners.";;
    Wed) echo "Attend group meeting.";;
    Thu) echo "Make plans for the weekend.";
         echo "Pick up clothes at the cleaners.";;
    Fri) echo "Answer E-mail.";;
    Sat) echo "You should not be here working.";
         echo "Finish your work and log off.";;
    Sun) echo "Call Grandma and Grandpa.";;
esac
```

To run this script, first use *chex* on the file:

```
$chex tickle RET
tickle is now executable:
-rwxrwx--x      1    yourlogin   457   Date time tickle
```

Now type the name of the file:

```
$tickle RET
```

This should print out the appropriate message for the day. However, we are not finished yet. A reminder service is not much good if you have to remember to type "tickle" to use it. It would be better to have the shell run the script automatically each time you log in. To do this, move the file *tickle* to your home directory:

```
$mv tickle $HOME RET
```

Next, use **vi** to open up your *.login* or *.profile* and insert the following line:

```
tickle
```

An Improved spell Program: *myspell*

The *spell* program is very useful, but it has a serious limitation: it lists the (possibly) misspelled words in a file, but does not tell you where in the file the misspelled words reside. Let's write a script that will correct this problem.

NAME
> *myspell*—an improved spelling-checker

SYNOPSIS
> ```
> spell filename
> ```

DESCRIPTION
> This is the pseudocode for *myspell*:

> > Select **sh**
> > Get the file name from the command line ($1)
> > Run spell on the file; for each misspelling
> > do
> > > Run **grep** to find the lines containing the misspellings
> > > Print the misspelled word
> > > Print the line(s) containing the misspellings
> > done

Open up a file named *myspell* and enter the following script:

```
#!/bin/sh
# An improved spelling-checker
file=$1
for word in `spell $file`
do
     line=`grep -n $word $file`
     echo "      "
     echo "Misspelled word: $word"
     echo "$line"
done
```

Next, use *chex* to make the script executable:

```
$chex myspell RET
myspell is now executable:
-rwxrwx--x      1    yourlogin   140   Date time myspell
```

You can use the program by typing the command with the name of the file to be checked:

```
$myspell file RET
```

Echo the Arguments Multiple Times: *echo.by*

The standard **echo** command echoes its arguments just once. The script presented here echoes the arguments as many times as the user chooses.

> NAME
> > *echo.by*—echo the arguments *n* times
>
> SYNOPSIS
> > ```
> > echo.by n arguments
> > ```
>
> DESCRIPTION
> > This is the pseudocode for *echo.by*
> >
> > > Select **sh**
> > > Get $count from the command line ($1)
> > > Use **shift** to get rid of the first argument
> > > Get the message from the command line ($*)
> > > While $count is greater than 0
> > > do
> > > > print the message
> > > > subtract 1 from $count
> > > done

Use the **vi** editor to create a file containing the following script:

```
#!/bin/sh
#Echo a line n times
count=$1
shift
message=$*
while test $count -gt 0
do
     echo $message
     count=`expr $count - 1`
done
```

Next, use *chex* to make the script executable:

```
$chex echo.by RET
echo.by is now executable:
-rwxrwx--x      1    yourlogin    111   Date time echo.by
```

You can use the script by typing *echo.by*, followed by the number of repetitions and the message to be echoed:

```
$echo.by 5 Play it again, Sam. RET
```

The first argument (5) will be read in, then the rest of the command line will be repeated 5 times:

```
Play it again, Sam.
Play it again, Sam.
Play it again, Sam.
Play it again, Sam.
Play it again, Sam.
```

Exercises

(1)* Write a shell script ***chnoex*** that reverses the effects of ***chex*** by removing the execution permissions on a file.

(2)* Write a shell script *private* that uses **chmod** to change the access permissions on a file so that only the owner may read, write, or execute it. Be sure to label the output to show what was done to the file.

(3)* Write a shell script *public* that reverses the effect of *private.*

(4)* Modify the *del* script so that it detects whether the user has specified a directory to be deleted. (Hint: use the **test** with the **−d** option to test for a directory.)

(5)* Rewrite *tickle* to use an **if/then/elif.../fi** structure.

(6)* Rewrite *echo.by* to use an **until** loop.

(7)* If you haven't already done so, write and run the sample shell scripts in the previous chapter.

Part VII
PROGRAMMING UNDER UNIX

18. Programming under UNIX

UNIX was originally written by professional programmers for the use of other professional programmers. It is not surprising, therefore, that UNIX provides a number of excellent programming tools. In this chapter, we will see how FORTRAN, Pascal, and C programs can be written and run under UNIX.

Programming Languages

A *computer program* is a set of coded instructions that tell the computer how to perform some task. Computers do not (yet) understand English or any other human language. Instead, computers respond to what is called *machine language,* in which everything is represented by binary numbers—combinations of 0s and 1s. Consider, for example, how a simple English phrase might appear in binary form:

```
1000101 1110110 1100101 1110010 1111001 1100010 1101111
   E       v       e       r       y       b       o

1100100 1111100 0100000 1101100 1101111 1110110 1100101
   d       y    [space]    l       o       v       e

1110011 0100000 1010101 1001110 1001001 1011000 0100001
   s    [space]    U       N       I       X       !
```

Here we have used the American National Standard Code for Information Interchange, usually called ASCII (ask-ee) code. Obviously, a binary code such as ASCII is very difficult for humans to understand. If you were forced to program in binary, you would find the job tedious at best. Fortunately, programming languages are available which, if they do not make programming easy, at least make it bearable. Every UNIX system comes equipped with the C programming language. (UNIX itself is written in C.) Some systems also offer the FORTRAN and Pascal languages as well.

Program Design

The first step is to design the program: plan what the program is to do, and how, and translate this plan into a computer language such as C or FORTRAN. This is the most important and the most difficult part of preparing a computer program. Entire volumes have been devoted to this topic; obviously, we can only scratch the surface in this short book.

The first step in program design is to define the problem to be solved. To illustrate the process, let's write a program to calculate the reciprocal of a number:

> **Problem:** Create a program to calculate the reciprocals of numbers entered
> by the user at the keyboard; display the results on the terminal screen.

A common tool used in program design is called *pseudocode*, which is a kind of outline of the program. Pseudocode is written in abbreviated English to resemble the structure of the actual program. The pseudocode for our reciprocal program might be:

> prompt the user for a number x
> read x
> calculate $1/x$
> display the answer

Source Code

Once you are satisfied with your program design, you can begin to write *source code* using a programming language. We will show you how the source code for the reciprocal program would appear in three different languages: C, FORTRAN and Pascal. However, we cannot in such a short book teach you much about any of these languages—you should consult a standard textbook for this.

Typically, you will use a text editor such as **vi** to prepare a file containing the source code. You will follow the usual naming rules for this file, but with one additional rule: files containing source code always have a suffix which indicates the language in which they are written. The suffix *.c* indicates a C-language source code, the suffix *.p* indicates a Pascal source code, and the suffix *.f* indicates FORTRAN code. Thus, for our program to compute reciprocals, we might have

> *recip.c*   (C version)
> *recip.p*   (Pascal version)
> *recip.f*   (FORTRAN version)

Compiling and Linking

Once you have finished the source code, you must translate it into machine language. This is called *compiling* the code, and the program that performs this task is called a *compiler*.

Some languages—such as C—pass your source code through a *preprocessor,* which makes certain substitutions and other changes. Then the altered code is sent to the compiler itself.

When the compiler sets to work on a file, one of two things can happen:

The compilation fails. Sometimes the source code contains errors that cannot be translated into machine language. Most compilers will give you an *error message* that explains what the error is and approximately where in the program it is found. You will have to use the **vi** editor to correct the error and then try to compile the program again.

The compilation succeeds. The compiler produces a file containing what is called *object code*. This is then passed to the *linker*, a program that combines your object code with code from the system libraries to produce a file of *executable code*.

Program Execution

The file containing the executable code is given the name *a.out* by the linker (unless you specify another name). To execute the program, all you have to do is to type

```
%a.out [RETURN]
```

If you want to save the executable code, you can use the **mv** command to give this file an appropriate name.

Debugging

Programs often contain errors ("bugs"). Errors that are found by the compiler are called *compilation errors*. These take time to locate and correct, but are usually pretty obvious. More insidious are the kind of errors that escape detection by the compiler. These are called *runtime errors* because they usually are not noticed until you run the program a few times.

Remember: Do not assume that a program is error-free just because it compiles and runs a few times without producing error messages. Beware the hidden bugs!

A serious runtime error, such as dividing by zero or taking the square root of a negative number, may cause the program to crash. The program quits running, and the UNIX shell sends you an error message of some sort. Usually, these messages are not very informative: they tell you that the program crashed, but they don't always tell you the reason.

When a program aborts because of a run-time error, the system produces a *core dump*, which is a file containing a "snapshot" of the main memory at the time the program failed. This is put into a file named *core*. The *core* file contains machine code, so it is not something you would try to read directly yourself. However, most UNIX systems include special programs called *debuggers* that are designed to help you exterminate bugs in your programs. A debugger can use the information in the *core* file to determine what the bug was and where it occurred. One debugger found on many UNIX systems is called **dbx**. This debugger is described in Appendix C.

One thing to remember about the *core* file is that it tends to be quite large, so you should delete it as soon as you can.

The make Utility

When writing large programs, it is the usual practice to divide the source code up among several different files. This allows different programmers to work on different parts of the program. It is also more efficient to change and recompile one part of the program at a time, rather than having to compile the entire program whenever a small change is made. The **make** program is used to keep track of the files making up a large program and to recompile parts of the program as needed. Although **make** is most often used with programs, it can also be useful in updating any project consisting of multiple files.

The lint Utility (C Programming Tool)

C is a very powerful language, but C compilers tend to be lax at checking for some kinds of errors. UNIX offers a tool called **lint** that can find errors that the compiler might miss. **lint** does not produce executable code. Instead, it examines your source code and prints warnings about potential problems. **lint** tends to be very picky and will often warn you about things that really aren't problems, but it also can spot things that you or the compiler would otherwise miss.

Exercises

None of these exercises requires the computer.

(1) Define: (a) computer program; (b) ASCII; (c) binary code; (d) pseudocode; (e) compiler; (f) source code; (g) preprocessor; (h) object code; (i) executable code; (j) linker; (k) debugger; (l) compilation error; (m) runtime error; (n) debugger; (o) core.

(2) Write pseudocode for a program to compute square roots.

19. Tutorial: Programming in C

C is the "native language" of UNIX—most of the UNIX operating system is written in C. It is not surprising, therefore, that for many applications C is the preferred language of UNIX programmers.

In this chapter, you will see how to take advantage of some of the features that make programming in C possible. This is not intended to teach you C; for that, you should consult a standard text on C. Indeed, it is a good idea to keep a C book handy as you read through this chapter.

Traditional First C Program

Use the **vi** editor to create a file named *hello.c*:

```
$vi hello.c RET
```

Next enter the following lines into the file:

```
/* Traditional first C program. */

#include <stdio.h>

main()
{
    printf("Hello, world!\n");
}
```

Let's examine this program in more detail:

- ```
  /* Traditional first C program. */
  ```

Any text appearing between `/*` and `*/` is considered a *comment* and is ignored by the compiler. Comments are included for the benefit of the programmer and anyone else who may read the program later.

- ```
  #include <stdio.h>
  ```

Lines that begin with a pound sign (#) in the first column are taken to be instructions to the preprocessor. These are usually called *preprocessor directives* or *control lines*. In this case, the control line tells the preprocessor to include the contents of the file *stdio.h* ("standard input/output header" file) in the program before it is compiled. The angle brackets < > tell the preprocessor to search for *stdio.h* in the "usual place," which for most UNIX systems is the directory */usr/include*. You can also tell the preprocessor to include files that you have written yourself, in which case you would surround the file's pathname by double quotes. Thus the control line

```
#include "myfile.h"
```

would include *myfile.h* in the program before it is compiled.

- `main()`

C programs consist of one or more units called *functions*. Every C program must include a function **main**, where execution begins. We know that **main** is the name of a function because of the parentheses.

- `{`

Each function body begins with a left brace. Braces are also used within the function body to group lines of code together.

- `printf("Hello, world!\n");`

printf is a standard C library function used to "print" output on the standard output. The argument to the function is a group of characters enclosed by double quotes, which is called a *string*. At the end of the string (but inside the double quotes) are the two characters \n, which together stand for a NEWLINE or RETURN. The entire line is terminated by a semicolon.

- `}`

The function body ends with a right brace, which matches the left brace at the beginning of the function body. The compiler will consider it an error if you omit this brace.

Compiling and Running *hello.c*

The standard C compiler is called *cc*. To compile the file, simply type *cc* followed by the name of the file. Remember that the file name must end in *.c*:

```
$cc hello.c RET
```

This command causes three things to happen:

(1) The C preprocessor goes through the file *hello.c* and looks for preprocessor directives to carry out. After making the changes, it passes the altered code to the compiler.

(2) The C compiler translates the C source code into object code, which it places in a file named *hello.o*.

(3) The linker combines your object code with any code your program may need from the standard libraries to produce executable code. In this case, the program uses the library function **printf**. The executable code is placed in a file named *a.out*, and the object file *hello.o* is deleted.

Note that the file containing the executable code is given the name *a.out* by the linker. To execute the program, all you have to do is to type

```
$a.out RET
```

You should see the message

```
Hello, world!
$
```

If you want to save the executable code, you can use the **mv** command to give this file an appropriate name. (If you don't do this, the executable file will be overwritten the next time you use the **cc** compiler.) It is common practice to give the executable code the same name as the source code, but without the *.c* suffix:

```
$mv a.out hello RET
```

Now you can run the program by typing *hello*:

```
$hello RET
Hello, world!
$
```

The *recip.c* Program

Our next program calculates reciprocals of numbers entered by the user at the keyboard. A pseudocode outline for this program might be

> Print a brief message about what the program does
> Prompt the user for a number *n*
> Read *n*
> Calculate 1/*n*
> Display the answer

Use the **vi** to create a file named ***recip.c***, and enter the following code into the file:

```
/* Compute reciprocals */

#include <stdio.h>

main()
{
    int n, recip;
    printf("This program computes reciprocals.\n");
    printf("Enter a number: ");
    scanf("%d", &n);
    recip = 1/n;
    printf("The reciprocal of %d is %d.\n", n, recip);
}
```

This program introduces a few new features that were not in the previous program:

-   `int n, recip;`

This is a *declaration* statement. It tells the compiler to create two variables to hold integers (**int**) and to give them the names n and `recip`. C requires that you declare all variables before you use them.

-   `scanf("%d", &n);`

scanf is a standard UNIX library function, used to get input from the standard input. This function has two arguments, `"%d"` and `&n`. `"%d"` is called a *control string*; it tells the compiler about the format of the input. In this case, the format specification `%d` stands for a single decimal integer. `&n` tells **scanf** to store the integer that it reads in the variable n. The ampersand (`&`) is the *address operator*; it is required in this context. (The most common **scanf** mistake is to omit the `&`.)

-   `recip = 1/n;`

This is how we compute the reciprocal. The computer first divides the integer 1 by the contents of the variable n, and then assigns the result to the variable `recip`. In C, = is called the *assignment operator*; it tells the computer to take the value of the expression on the right and assign it to the variable on the left.

-   `printf("The reciprocal of %d is %d.\n", n, recip);`

This is another **printf** function, with a difference. There are three arguments this time, instead of one. The first argument is a string containing two formats (`%d` and `%d`). The other two arguments are variables (n and `recip`). The **printf** function prints out the string, substituting the contents of n and `recip` for the two formats.

Compiling and Running *recip.c*

We saw before that the default name for an executable file is *a.out*. You can specify another name using **cc** with the **–o** option. For the executable, let's use the name *recip* (without the *.c* suffix):

    §`cc -o recip recip.c` `RET`

This tells **cc** to compile *recip.c* and put the executable in the file *recip*. To run the program, type the name of the executable file and press RETURN. Enter a 0 at the prompt:

    §`recip` `RET`
    `This program computes reciprocals.`
    `Enter a number: 0` `RET`

You should receive an error message, something like

    `Arithmetic exception (core dumped)`

What happened? It actually isn't too hard to figure out: entering a zero caused a division by zero, which is not allowed. The program then crashed, creating a *core* file. Since you cannot read a *core* file, and because it takes up so much room, you should delete it:

```
$rm core RET
```

Setting up the Program for Debugging

Although you cannot read the core directly yourself, you can use a *debugger* such as **dbx** to examine the core dump and determine what caused the program to crash. Before you can do this, however, you must compile the program using the **–g** option:

```
$cc -g recip.c
```

This causes the compiler to include additional information in the compiled code that can be used by **dbx**. If you would like to see how **dbx** is used, please refer to Appendix C.

Integer Division

Division by zero does not work; what about other numbers? Let's try to compute the reciprocal of 2:

```
$recip RET
This program computes reciprocals.
Enter a number: 2 RET
```

You should see the output

```
The reciprocal of 2 is 0.
```

This obviously is not right. Let's try it with the input 3:

```
$recip RET
This program computes reciprocals.
Enter a number: 3 RET
```

You should see

```
The reciprocal of 3 is 0.
```

Try it again with the input of 1:

```
$recip RET
This program computes reciprocals.
Enter a number: 1 RET
```

You should see

```
The reciprocal of 1 is 1.
```

This program only works with 1 as an input. The reason has to do with the way that the computer stores and uses integers. To repair this defect, you should revise the program to use variables of type **float** or **double** rather than type **int**.

The *sqroot.c* Program

Our next program calculates the square roots of numbers entered by the user at the keyboard. A pseudocode outline for this program might be

> Print a brief message about what the program does
> Prompt the user for a number *n*
> Read *n*
> Compute the square root of *n*
> Display the answer

Use the **vi** to create a file named *sqroot.c*, and enter the following code into the file:

```
/* Compute square roots */

#include <stdio.h>
#include <math.h>

main()
{
    double n, root;
    printf("This program computes square roots.\n");
    printf("Enter a number: ");
    scanf("%lf", &n);
    root = sqrt(n);
    printf("The square root of %d is %d.\n", n, root);
}
```

This program introduces some new elements:

- ```
  #include <math.h>
  ```

This control line tells the preprocessor to include the contents of the file *math.h* (standard math header file) in the program before it is compiled. As before, the angle brackets < > tell the preprocessor to search for the file in the "usual place," most likely the directory */usr/include*.

- ```
  double n, root;
  ```

This declaration statement tells the compiler to create two variables to hold **double** values and to give them the names n and root.

- ```
  scanf("%lf", &n);
  ```

The control string in this **scanf** contains the format specification %lf, which stands for "long float," a synonym for **double**.

- ```
  root = sqrt(n);
  ```

This statement uses the library function **sqrt** to compute the square root of n and assigns the result to the variable root.

Compiling and Running *sqroot.c*

The program *sqroot.c* uses the math library function **sqrt**. The **–lm** option tells the compiler to include the standard the math library when the program is compiled:

```
$cc -o sqroot sqroot.c -lm RET
```

Note that the **–lm** option comes at the end of the command line because it is really an instruction to the linker to use the math library code. To run the program, type *sqroot* and press RETURN:

```
$sqroot RET
This program computes square roots.
```

Then enter a 4 at the prompt:

```
Enter a number: 4 RET
```

You should see

```
The square root of 4 is 2.
$
```


Multiple Source Files

Our last sample program illustrates the use of separate source files for putting together a large program. Large programs are often the work of more than one programmer; it is common for each programmer to work on his or her own files, which then are assembled to make a complete program.

Create a directory named *Trip* and move to the new directory:

```
$mkdir Trip RET
$cd Trip RET
```

Use the **vi** editor to open up a new file named *main.c*, and enter the following code:

```
main ()
{
     chicago();
     indiana();
     chicago();
}
```

Compiling without Linking

main is a simple function. All it does is call two other functions, **indiana** and **chicago**. We have not yet written these two functions, so the program is not complete. Nevertheless, we can still run *main.c* through the compiler to check for compiler errors using **cc** with the **-c** option:

```
$cc -c main.c RET
```

If the compilation is successful, this creates a file named *main.o*. On the other hand, if the compiler detects an error in the file, it will give you an error message, and no object file is created. (If there are errors in the file, correct them now and recompile using *cc -c*.)

Creating and Compiling *chicago.c*

Next open up a file named *chicago.c* and enter the following lines of code:

```
void chicago()
{
     printf("\nI'm waiting at O'Hare International,\n");
     printf("the busiest airport in the world.\n");
}
```

Check this for compilation errors by using *cc -c* on the file:

```
$cc -c chicago.c RET
```

Creating and Compiling *indiana.c*

Now use the **vi** editor to create a file named *indiana.c*, and enter the following code:

```
void indiana()
{
     printf("\nBack home again, Indiana.\n");
     indianapolis();
     printf("\nWander Indiana-come back soon.\n");
}
```

Use the *cc -c* command to compile this function:

```
$cc -c indiana.c RET
```

Creating and Compiling *indy.c*

There is still one more function to write. Use the editor to create a file *indy.c*:

```
#define POP90  1.2       /* Population in millions */
void indianapolis()
{
        printf("Welcome to Indianapolis, Indiana.\n");
        printf("Population: %f million.\n", POP90);
}
```

The first line of this program begins with a pound sign (#), indicating a preprocessor directive. It tells the preprocessor to search through the file and replace every occurrence of the string POP90 with 1.2, the population (in millions) of Indianapolis in 1990. Compile this function with the *cc –c* command:

$cc -c indy.c RET

Compiling and Running the *Trip* Program

If you have done everything correctly, you should now have five files of C source code and five files of object code in the directory *Trip*. Check this with the **ls** command:

$ls RET

You should see something like this:

```
chicago.c      indiana.c      indy.c      main.c
chicago.o      indiana.o      indy.o      main.o
```

All that you need to do now is to link these files together to make an executable file. This command will do the trick:

$cc *.o RET

This will create an executable named *a.out*. To run the program, simply type

$a.out RET

The output will be something like this:

```
I'm waiting at O'Hare International,
the busiest airport in the world.

Back home again, Indiana.

Welcome to Indianapolis, Indiana.
Population: 1.20000 million.
```

```
Wander Indiana--come back soon.

I'm waiting at O'Hare International,
the busiest airport in the world.
```

Maintaining a Program with make

One advantage to breaking up a large program into multiple source files is that it allows you to modify and recompile one source file without having to recompile the entire program. The UNIX **make** program is useful in keeping track of the changes you make in the program files.

The **make** program looks for its instructions in a file named either *makefile* or *Makefile*. For the program in the *Trip* directory, create a file named *makefile*, and enter the following lines:

```
# Makefile for the Trip program

trip: main.o chicago.o indiana.o indy.o
TAB cc -o trip main.o chicago.o indiana.o indy.o

chicago.o: chicago.c
TAB cc -c chicago.c

indiana.o: indiana.c
TAB cc -c indiana.c

indy.o: indy.c
TAB cc -c indy.c

clean:
TAB rm *.o
```

Let's consider some of the interesting features of this file:

•   `# Makefile for the Trip program`

This is a comment line. **make** ignores anything that follows a pound sign (#).

•   `trip: main.o chicago.o indiana.o indy.o`

This is a called a *dependency line*. It indicates that the file *trip* depends on the object files *main.o*, *chicago.o*, *indiana.o*, and *indy.o*. Note that the dependency line must begin in the first column.

- ☐TAB cc -o trip main.o chicago.o indiana.o indy.o

This is an *action line*. It follows the dependency line and shows how the file *trip* is created from the files *main.o*, *chicago.o*, *indiana.o*, and *indy.o*. In this case, **cc** links the object files and puts the executable into *trip*. Action lines must begin with a tab.

- chicago.o: chicago.c

This is another dependency line, showing that *chicago.o* depends on the source file *chicago.c*.

- ☐TAB cc -c chicago.c

This is an action line, showing that *chicago.o* is produced by compiling *chicago.c* using **cc** with the **–c** option.

- clean:

This dependency line indicates that "clean" does not depend on any file. It is an example of an *empty dependency*. In this case, "clean" is not the name of a file, but rather a command, which you would run by typing

$make clean RET

make will then look through *makefile*, find the empty dependency "clean," and run the command on the next action line.

- [TAB]rm *.o

This action line will remove any files ending in *.o*—in other words, the object files. This is the action that **make** will perform when you type

$make clean RET

Using make

The first thing to do with **make** is to remove the executable and object files that were produced when you compiled the *Trip* program the first time. Try the **ls** command to see the files in *Trip*:

$ls RET

You should see something like this:

```
a.out          indiana.c      indy.o      main.o
chicago.c      indiana.o      main.c      makefile
chicago.o      indy.c
```

Now get rid of the old object files:

```
$make clean RET
```

The "clean" dependency line in *makefile* causes the following command line to run:

```
rm *.o
```

Use the **ls** command now to list the files remaining in *Trip*:

```
$ls RET
```

You should see:

```
a.out          indiana.c      main.c
chicago.c      indy.c         makefile
```

Note that **make** did nothing to the old executable file *a.out*, because it was not instructed to do so.

Next use **make** to compile the program. Simply type *make* and press RETURN:

```
$make RET
```

make then follows the instructions in *makefile* to compile the program:

```
cc -c main.c
cc -c chicago.c
cc -c indiana.c
cc -c indy.c
cc -o trip main.o chicago.o indiana.o indy.o
```

Note that the files are not necessarily compiled in exactly the same order as they appear in *makefile*. **make** figures out which files should be compiled first. Try the **ls** command to see the files in *Trip*:

```
$ls RET
```

You should see something like this:

```
a.out          indiana.c      indy.o      makefile
chicago.c      indiana.o      main.c      trip
chicago.o      indy.c         main.o
```

trip contains the new executable code, which you can run simply by typing *trip*, followed by RETURN:

```
$trip RET
```

The advantage of using **make** to compile the files becomes apparent when you begin making alterations in any of the source files. When you are finished, all you have to do is type *make*, and **make** will automatically recompile only those files that need it. And if you have not made any changes in the program, **make** will take no action. To see how this works, try running **make** again:

$make RET

Assuming you have not made any changes in the files, you should see a message such as

'trip' is up to date. RET

Summary

Each of these commands is typed after the shell prompt and is terminated by a RETURN.

Compiling and Linking

cc *file.c*	compile and link the source code in *file.c*
cc -c *file.c*	compile *file.c* but do not link; put output in *file.o*
cc -g *file.c*	compile and link *file.c*; set up for the debugger
cc -o *outfile file.c*	compile and link *file.c* place output in *outfile*
cc *file.c* -o *outfile*	same as previous command
cc *file.c* -lm	compile *file.c* and link with code from the standard math library

Using make

make	update the files according to rules and actions specified in *makefile* or *Makefile*
make *xyz*	perform the action specified by the empty dependency *xyz* in *makefile* or *Makefile*

Exercises

The exercises marked with an asterisk (*) are intended to be done at the keyboard.

(1)   Define (a) comment; (b) preprocessor directive; (c) control line; (d) function; (e) string; (f) declaration; (g) control string; (h) assignment operator; (i) dependency line; (j) action line.

(2)* The UNIX program **lint** is used to check source code for possible errors. To run **lint** on the source file *file.c*, type the command line

$lint *file.c* RET

Run **lint** on each of the C source files you created in this chapter, and note the kinds of messages it gives you.

(3)* Rewrite *recip.c* to employ **double** or **float** variables.

(4)* Refer to your C book to see how to format the output from **printf.** Revise *recip.c* using the `%f`, `%e`, and/or `%g` formats to control the spacing of the output line.

(5)* Revise *indy.c* to control spacing in the output line; then use the **make** command to recompile the *Trip.c* program.

(6)* Even if you have rewritten *recip.c* to use **double** or **float** data, it may still not handle an input of zero correctly. Read your C book about the **if–then** statement, then rewrite the *recip.c* program so that it prints the message "The reciprocal of 0 is not defined" if the user types in a zero.

(7)* The **system** function allows a C program to execute UNIX commands. For example, the statement

```
system("date");
```

runs the UNIX **date** command. Rewrite the *hello.c* program so that it displays the date, then lists the files in your home directory and the users logged into the system.

20. Tutorial: Programming in FORTRAN

FORTRAN ("FORmula TRANslation") was one of the first and most successful programming languages. Although it was developed in the 1950s, it has been repeatedly upgraded over the years, and it is still popular with scientists and engineers. The most widely used version of FORTRAN is called FORTRAN 77. It is not a standard part of UNIX, but it is often found on larger UNIX systems.

In this chapter, you will see how to write, compile, and run FORTRAN 77 programs on a UNIX system. This is not intended to teach you FORTRAN; for that, you should consult a standard text on FORTRAN. Indeed, it is a good idea to keep a FORTRAN book handy as you read through this chapter.

First FORTRAN Program

Use the **vi** editor to create a file named *hello.f*:

```
$vi hello.f RET
```

Next enter the following lines into the file:

```
* First FORTRAN program.
*234567

      PROGRAM HELLO
      WRITE(*,*) 'Hello, world!'
      END.
```

Let's examine this program in more detail:

- ```
  * First FORTRAN program.
  ```

Any line of text that begins with an asterisk (*) in the first column is treated as a *comment* and is ignored by the compiler. Comments are for the benefit of the programmer and anyone else who may read the program later.

- ```
  *234567
  ```

This is another comment line, included to help you identify the first seven columns. FORTRAN 77 requires statements to begin in the seventh column.

- ```
  PROGRAM HELLO
  ```

The **PROGRAM** statement marks the beginning of the program and gives the program a name (HELLO). Traditionally, FORTRAN statements have been written entirely in uppercase letters, and this practice continues, although many FORTRAN compilers also will accept lowercase letters. Thus, on many compilers the **PROGRAM** statement could also be written as

```
      program hello
```
```

-     `WRITE(*,*) 'Hello, world!'`

The **WRITE** statement is used to print output on the screen.

-     `END`

The **END** statement marks the end of the program.

Compiling and Running *hello.f*

Since FORTRAN is not a standard part of the UNIX system, FORTRAN compilers go under different names. Perhaps the most common name used for the FORTRAN compiler is **f77**. Try typing *f77* followed by the name of the file. Remember that the file name must end in *.f*

    $f77 hello.f`RET`

This command causes three things to happen:

(1)   The FORTRAN 77 compiler goes through the file **hello.f** and makes certain substitutions specified by the PARAMETER statements, if there are any.

(2)   The FORTRAN 77 compiler translates the FORTRAN source code into object code, which it places in a file named **hello.o**.

(3)   The linker combines your object code with any code your program may need from the UNIX standard libraries to produce executable code. The executable code is placed in a file named **a.out**, and the object file **hello.o** is deleted.

Note that the file containing the executable code is given the name **a.out** by the linker. To execute the program, all you have to do is to type

    $a.out`RET`

You should see the message

    `Hello, world!`
    $

If you want to save the executable code, you can use the **mv** command to give this file an appropriate name. (If you don't do this, the executable file will be overwritten the next time you use the **cc** compiler.) It is common practice to give the executable code the same name as the source code, but without the *.f* suffix:

    $mv a.out hello`RET`

Now you can run the program by typing *hello*:

```
$hello RET
Hello, world!
$
```

The *recip.f* Program

Our next program calculates reciprocals of numbers entered by the user at the keyboard. A pseudocode outline for this program might be

> Print a brief message about what the program does
> Prompt the user for a number *n*
> Read *n*
> Calculate 1/*n*
> Display the answer

Use **vi** to create a file named *recip.f*, and enter the following code into the file:

```
C Compute reciprocals
C234567

      PROGRAM RECIPROCAL

      INTEGER N, RECIP;

      WRITE(*,*) 'This program computes reciprocals.'
      WRITE(*,*) 'Enter a number: '

      READ(*,*) N

      RECIP = 1/N

      WRITE(*,*) 'The reciprocal of ', N, ' is ', RECIP

      END
```

This program introduces a few new features that were not in the previous program:

- `C Compute reciprocals`

An alternative way to indicate a comment line is to place a capital *C* in the first column.

- `PROGRAM RECIPROCAL`

The program name is `RECIPROCAL`. Note, however, that many FORTRAN compilers recognize only the first six characters of a variable or program name. Such a compiler would treat these names as equivalent to `RECIPROCAL`:

```
      RECIPR
      RECIPRO
      RECIPROCALS
```

- `INTEGER N, RECIP`

This is a *declaration* statement. It tells the compiler to create two variables to hold integers and to give them the names N and RECIP.

- `READ(*,*) N`

This statement reads the user's input and stores it in the variable N. This is an example of *unformatted*, or *list-directed input*. You can also specify *formatted* input, in which case the asterisks (*,*) would be replaced by formatting instructions.

- `RECIP = 1/N`

This statement computes the reciprocal. The computer first divides the integer 1 by the contents of the variable N and then assigns the result to the variable RECIP.

- `WRITE(*,*) 'The reciprocal of ', N, ' is ', RECIP`

This **WRITE** statement prints out the string `'The reciprocal of '`, then the contents of N, then the string `' is '`, followed by the contents of RECIP.

Compiling and Running *recip.f*

We saw before that the default name for an executable file is *a.out*. You can specify another name using **f77** with the **–o** option. For the executable, let's use the name *recip* (without the *.f* suffix):

```
$f77 -o recip recip.f RET
```

This tells **f77** to compile *recip.f* and put the executable in the file *recip*. To run the program, type the name of the executable file and press RETURN. Enter a 0 at the prompt:

```
$recip RET
This program computes reciprocals.
Enter a number: 0 RET
```

You should receive an error message, something like

```
Arithmetic exception (core dumped)
```

What happened? It actually isn't too hard to figure out: entering a zero caused a division by zero, which is not allowed. The program then crashed, creating a *core* file. Since you cannot read a *core* file, and because it takes up so much room, you should delete it:

```
$rm core RET
```

Setting up the Program for Debugging

Although you cannot read the core directly yourself, you can use a *debugger* such as **dbx** to examine the core dump and determine what caused the program to crash. Before you can do this, however, you must compile the program using the **–g** option:

```
$f77 -g recip.f
```

This causes the compiler to include additional information in the compiled code that can be used by a debugger. If you would like to see how **dbx** is used, please refer to Appendix C.

Integer Division

Division by zero does not work; what about other numbers? Let's try to compute the reciprocal of 2:

```
$recip RET
This program computes reciprocals.
Enter a number: 2 RET
```

You should see the output

```
The reciprocal of   2 is   0
```

This obviously is not right. Try it again with the input 3:

```
$recip RET
This program computes reciprocals.
Enter a number: 3 RET
```

You should see

```
The reciprocal of   3 is   0
```

Try it again with the input of 1:

```
$recip RET
This program computes reciprocals.
Enter a number: 1 RET
```

You should see

```
The reciprocal of   1 is   1
```

This program only works with 1 as an input. The reason has to do with the way that the computer stores and uses integers. To repair this defect, you should revise the program to use variables of type **REAL** rather than type **INTEGER**.

Multiple Source Files

Our last sample program illustrates the use of separate source files for putting together a large program. Large programs are often the work of more than one programmer; it is common for each programmer to work on his or her own files, which then are assembled to make a complete program.

Create a directory named *Trip.f* and move to this new directory:

```
$mkdir Trip.f RET
$cd Trip.f RET
```

Use the **vi** editor to open up the file *main.f* and enter the following code into the file:

```
*234567
      PROGRAM MAIN
      CALL CHICAGO()
      CALL INDIANA()
      CALL CHICAGO()
      END
```

Write these lines into the file and quit the editor.

Compiling without Linking

The program MAIN simply calls two subroutines, CHICAGO and INDIANA, which have not yet been written. Nevertheless, we can still run *main.f* through the compiler to check for compiler errors using **cc** with the **–c** option:

```
$f77 -c main.f RET
```

If the compilation is successful, this creates a file named *main.o* . On the other hand, if the compiler detects an error in the file, it will give you an error message, and no object file is created. (If there are errors in the file, correct them now and recompile using *f77 –c*.)

Creating and Compiling *chicago.f*

Next open up a file named *chicago.f* and enter the following lines of code:

```
*234567

      SUBROUTINE CHICAGO()
      WRITE(*,*)'I''m waiting at O''Hare International
     +the busiest airport in the world.'
      END
```

There are two interesting features to note about the **WRITE** system in this program:

```
•      WRITE(*,*) 'I''m waiting at O''Hare International
```

Single quotes or apostrophes ('. . .') are placed around a string. If you want to include a single quote or apostrophe as part of the string, you must place *two* single quotes together. (Note that these are two single quotes, not a double quote symbol.)

```
•      +the busiest airport in the world.'
```

Any character other than a space or a zero placed in the sixth column of a FORTRAN line indicates that it is a *continuation* of the previous line. This is useful because FORTRAN statements are not allowed to extend beyond column 72.

Check *chicago.f* for compilation errors by using *f77 −c* on the file:

```
$f77 -c chicago.f RET
```

Creating and Compiling *indiana.f*

Now use the **vi** editor to create a file named *indiana.f*, and enter the following code:

```
*234567
       SUBROUTINE INDIANA
       WRITE(*,*) 'Back home again, Indiana.'
       CALL INDY()
       WRITE(*,*) 'Come back soon and wander Indiana.'
       END
```

Use the *f77 −c* command to compile this function:

```
$f77 -c indiana.f RET
```

Creating and Compiling *indy.f*

There is still one more function to write. Use the editor to create a file *indy.f*:

```
PARAMETER  POP90  1.2

*234567
       SUBROUTINE INDY()
       WRITE(*,*) 'Welcome to Indianapolis, Indiana.'
       WRITE(*,*) 'Population: ', POP90, ' million.'
       END
```

The first line of this program is a PARAMETER statement. The FORTRAN compiler will search through the file and replace every occurrence of the string POP90 with 1.2, the population (in millions) of Indianapolis in 1990. Compile this function with the *f77 −c* command:

```
$f77 -c indy.f RET
```

Compiling and Running the Program

If you have done everything correctly, you should now have five files of FORTRAN 77 source code and five files of object code in the directory *Trip.f*. Check this with the **ls** command:

```
$ls RET
```

You should see something like this:

```
chicago.f      indiana.f      indy.f      main.f
chicago.o      indiana.o      indy.o      main.o
```

All that you need to do now is to link these files together to make an executable file. This command will do the trick:

```
$f77 *.o RET
```

This will create an executable named *a.out*. To run the program, simply type

```
$a.out RET
```

The output will be something like this:

```
I'm waiting at O'Hare International,
the busiest airport in the world.

Back home again, Indiana.

Welcome to Indianapolis, Indiana.
Population: 1.20000 million.

Come back soon and wander Indiana.

I'm waiting at O'Hare International,
the busiest airport in the world.
```

Maintaining a Program with make

One advantage to breaking up a large program into multiple source files is that it allows you to modify and recompile one source file without having to recompile the entire program. The UNIX **make** program is useful in keeping track of the changes you make in the program files.

The **make** program looks for its instructions in a file named either *makefile* or *Makefile*. For the program in the *Trip.f* directory, create a file named *makefile*, and enter the following lines:

```
# Makefile for the Trip program

trip: main.o chicago.o indiana.o indy.o
TAB f77 -o trip main.o chicago.o indiana.o indy.o

chicago.o: chicago.f
TAB f77 -c chicago.f

indiana.o: indiana.f
TAB f77 -c indiana.f

indy.o: indy.f
TAB f77 -c indy.f

clean:
TAB rm *.o
```

Let's consider some of the interesting features of this file:

- `# Makefile for the Trip program`

This is a comment line. **make** ignores anything that follows a pound sign (#).

- `trip: main.o chicago.o indiana.o indy.o`

This is a called a *dependency line*. It indicates that the file *trip* depends on the object files *main.o*, *chicago.o*, *indiana.o*, and *indy.o*. Note that the dependency line must begin in the first column.

- `TAB f77 -o trip main.o chicago.o indiana.o indy.o`

This is an *action line*. It follows the dependency line and shows how the file *trip* is created from the files *main.o*, *chicago.o*, *indiana.o*, and *indy.o*. In this case, **f77** links the object files and puts the executable into *trip*. Action lines must begin with a tab.

- `chicago.o: chicago.f`

This is another dependency line, showing that *chicago.o* depends on the source file *chicago.f*.

- `TAB f77 -c chicago.f`

This is an action line, showing that *chicago.o* is produced by compiling *chicago.f* using **f77** with the **-c** option.

-     `clean:`

This dependency line indicates that "clean" does not depend on any file. It is an example of an *empty dependency*. In this case, "clean" is not the name of a file, but rather a command, which you would run by typing

        $make clean`RET`

make will then look through *makefile*, find the empty dependency "clean," and run the command on the next action line.

-     `TAB`rm *.o

This action line will remove any files ending in *.o*—in other words, the object files. This is the action that **make** will perform when you type

        $make clean`RET`

Using make

The first thing to do with **make** is to remove the executable and object files that were produced when you compiled the *Trip.f* program the first time. Try the **ls** command to see the files in *Trip.f*:

    $ls`RET`

You should see something like this:

```
a.out           indiana.f       indy.o      main.o
chicago.f       indiana.o       main.f      makefile
chicago.o       indy.f
```

Now get rid of the old object files:

    $make clean`RET`

The "clean" dependency line in *makefile* causes the following command line to run:

    `rm *.o`

Use the **ls** command now to list the files remaining in *Trip.f*:

    $ls`RET`

You should see:

```
a.out           indiana.f       main.f
chicago.f       indy.f          makefile
```

Note that **make** did nothing to the old executable file *a.out* because it was not instructed to do so.

Next use **make** to compile the program. Simply type *make* and press RETURN:

$make RET

make then follows the instructions in *makefile* to compile the program:

```
f77 -c main.f
f77 -c chicago.f
f77 -c indiana.f
f77 -c indy.f
f77 -o trip main.o chicago.o indiana.o indy.o
```

Note that the files are not necessarily compiled in exactly the same order as they appear in *makefile* because **make** figures out which files should be compiled first. Try the **ls** command to see the files in *Trip.f*:

$ls RET

You should see something like this:

```
a.out          indiana.f      indy.o     makefile
chicago.f      indiana.o      main.f     trip
chicago.o      indy.f         main.o
```

trip contains the new executable code, which you can run simply by typing *trip*, followed by RETURN:

$trip RET

The advantage of using **make** to compile the files becomes apparent when you begin making alterations in any of the source files. When you are finished, all you have to do is type *make*, and **make** will automatically recompile only those files that need it. And if you have not made any changes in the program, **make** will take no action. To see how this works, try running **make** again:

$make RET

Assuming you have not made any changes in the files, you should see a message such as

```
'trip' is up to date. RET
```

Summary

Each of these commands is typed after the shell prompt and is terminated by a RETURN.

Compiling and Linking

`f77 file.f`	compile and link the source code in *file.f*
`f77 -c file.f`	compile *file.f* but do not link; put output in *file.o*
`f77 -g file.f`	compile and link *file.f*; set up for the debugger
`f77 -o outfile file.f`	compile and link *file.f* place output in *outfile*
`f77 file.f -o outfile`	same as previous command
`f77 file.f -lm`	compile *file.f* and link with code from the standard math library

Using make

`make`	update the files according to rules and actions specified in *makefile* or *Makefile*
`make xyz`	perform the action specified by the empty dependency *xyz* in *makefile* or *Makefile*

Exercises

The exercises marked with an asterisk (*) are intended to be done at the keyboard.

(1) Define (a) comment; (b) PARAMETER statement; (c) PROGRAM statement; (d) END statement; (e) string; (f) declaration; (g) control string; (h) dependency line; (i) action line.

(2)* Rewrite *recip.f* to use **REAL** data.

(3)* The output from *recip.f* is not as attractive as it might be because of the spaces preceding the numbers. Refer to your FORTRAN book to see how to format the output; then revise *recip.f* to control the spacing of the output line.

(4)* Revise *indy.f* to control spacing in the output line; then use the **make** command to recompile the *Trip.f* program.

(5)* Even after rewriting *recip.f* to use **REAL** data, it may still not handle an input of zero correctly. Read your FORTRAN book about the **if-then** statement; then modify the *recip.f* program so that it prints the message "The reciprocal of 0 is not defined" if the user types in a zero.

(6)* Write a FORTRAN program *sqroot.f* to compute the square roots of numbers entered by the user at the keyboard.

21. Tutorial: Programming in Pascal

Pascal was developed by Niklaus Wirth during the late 1960s and early 1970s for teaching good programming style. It has since become one of the most popular computer languages. Although Pascal is not a standard part of UNIX, it is found on many UNIX systems.

In this chapter, you will see how to write, compile, and run Pascal programs. This is not intended to teach you Pascal; for that, you should consult a standard text on Pascal. Indeed, it is a good idea to keep a Pascal book handy as you read through this chapter.

Traditional First Pascal Program

Use the **vi** editor to create a file named *hello.p*:

```
$vi hello.p RET
```

Next enter the following lines into the file:

```
(* Traditional first Pascal program. *)

program HelloWorld(output);
begin
    writeln('Hello, world!')
end.
```

Let's examine this program in more detail:

•   `(* Traditional first Pascal program. *)`

Any text appearing between (* and *) is a *comment* and is ignored by the compiler. Comments are included for the benefit of the programmer and anyone else who may read the program later.

•   `program HelloWorld(output);`

Every Pascal program must begin with the word **program**, which is a *reserved word* in Pascal. This means that **program** has a predefined meaning in Pascal and cannot be used any other way by the programmer. Every program must also have a *name* or *identifier*—in this case, `HelloWorld`. The semicolon at the end of the line is used to separate statements.

•   `begin`

The beginning of the program body is indicated by the reserved word **begin**.

- ```
  writeln('Hello, world!');
  ```

writeln is a standard Pascal procedure used to "write" a line output on the standard output. The argument to the procedure is a group of characters enclosed by single quotes, which is called a *string*.

- ```
  end.
  ```

The program body ends with the reserved word **end**, followed by a period (.).

Compiling and Running *hello.p*

Pascal compilers on UNIX systems go under different names, the most common being **pc**. To compile the program using **pc**, simply type *pc* followed by the name of the file. Remember that the file name must end in *.p*:

$pc hello.p RET

This command causes the Pascal compiler to translate source code into object code, which it places in a file named *hello.o*. The linker then combines your object code with any code your program may need from the standard libraries to produce executable code. The executable code is placed in a file named *a.out*, and the object file *hello.o* is deleted.

The file containing the executable code is given the name *a.out* by the linker. To execute the program, all you have to do is to type

$a.out RET

You should see the message

```
Hello, world!
$
```

If you want to save the executable code, you can use the **mv** command to give this file an appropriate name. (If you don't do this, the executable file will be overwritten the next time you use the **pc** compiler.) It is common practice to give the executable code the same name as the source code, but without the *.p* suffix:

$mv a.out hello RET

Now you can run the program by typing *hello*:

```
$hello RET
Hello, world!
$
```

The *recip.p* Program

Our next program calculates reciprocals of numbers entered by the user at the keyboard. A pseudocode outline for this program might be

> Print a brief message about what the program does
> Prompt the user for a number *n*
> Read *n*
> Calculate 1/*n*
> Display the answer

Use the **vi** to create a file named *recip.p*, and enter the following code into the file:

```
{ Compute reciprocals }

program reciprocal(input, output)
var n, recip: integer;
begin
    writeln('This program computes reciprocals.');
    write('Enter a number: ');
    readln(n);
    recip := 1 div n;
    writeln('The reciprocal of ', n, ' is ', recip)
end.
```

This program introduces a few new features that were not in the previous program:

-    `{ Compute reciprocals }`

This shows an alternative way to write comments: surround the comment with braces {...}.

-    `var n, recip: integer;`

This is a *declaration* statement. It tells the compiler to create two variables (**var**) to hold integers, and to give them the names n and `recip`. Pascal requires that you declare all variables before you use them. A semicolon is placed at the end of this statement to separate it from those that follow.

-    `write('Enter a number: ');`

write is a standard Pascal procedure, used to write output on the standard output. Unlike **writeln, write** does not start a new line on the screen.

-    `readln(n);`

This **readln** statement obtains the user's input from the standard input and stores it in the variable n.

- ```
    recip := 1 div n;
  ```

This line computes the reciprocal. The computer first divides the integer 1 by the contents of the variable n, then assigns the result to the variable `recip`. In Pascal, **div** is used for dividing two integers. The pair of symbols := is treated as one operator, called the *assignment operator*. It assigns the value of the expression 1 div n to the variable `recip`.

- ```
    writeln('The reciprocal of ', n, ' is ', recip)
  ```

This is a **writeln** with four arguments. It will print out the string `'The reciprocal of '`, followed by the *value* of the variable n, the string `' is '`, and finally the value of the variable `recip`.

Compiling and Running *recip.p*

We saw before that the default name for an executable file is ***a.out***. You can specify another name using **pc** with the **–o** option. For the executable, let's use the name ***recip*** (without the *.p* suffix):

```
$pc -o recip recip.p RET
```

This tells **pc** to compile ***recip.p*** and put the executable in the file ***recip***. To run the program, type the name of the executable file and press RETURN. Enter a 0 at the prompt:

```
$recip RET
This program computes reciprocals.
Enter a number: 0 RET
```

You should receive an error message, something like

```
Arithmetic exception (core dumped)
```

What happened? It actually isn't too hard to figure out: entering a zero caused a division by zero, which is not allowed. The program then crashed, creating a ***core*** file. Since you cannot read a ***core*** file, and because it takes up so much room, you should delete it:

```
$rm core RET
```

Setting up the Program for Debugging

Although you cannot read the core directly yourself, you can use a *debugger* such as **dbx** to examine the core dump and determine what caused the program to crash. Before you can do this, however, you must compile the program using the **–g** option:

```
$pc -g recip.p
```

This causes the compiler to include additional information in the compiled code that can be used by **dbx**. If your system has this debugger, and you would like to see how it is used, please refer to Appendix C.

Integer Division

Division by zero does not work; what about other numbers? Let's try to compute the reciprocal of 2:

```
$recip RET
This program computes reciprocals.
Enter a number: 2 RET
```

You should see the output

```
The reciprocal of          2 is          0.
```

This obviously is not right. Let's try it with the input 3:

```
$recip RET
This program computes reciprocals.
Enter a number: 3 RET
```

You should see

```
The reciprocal of          3 is          0.
```

Try it again with the input of 1:

```
$recip RET
This program computes reciprocals.
Enter a number: 1 RET
```

You should see

```
The reciprocal of          1 is          1.
```

This program only works with 1 as an input. The reason has to do with the way that the computer stores and uses integers. To repair this defect, you should revise the program to use variables of type **real** rather than type **integer**.

Summary

Each of these commands is typed after the shell prompt, and is terminated by a RETURN.

Compiling and Linking

`pc file.p`	compile and link the source code in *file.p*
`pc -c file.p`	compile *file.p* but do not link; put output in *file.o*
`pc -g file.p`	compile and link *file.p*; set up for the debugger
`pc -o outfile file.p`	compile and link *file.p*; place output in *outfile*
`pc file.p -o outfile`	same as previous command

Exercises

The exercises marked with an asterisk (*) are intended to be done at the keyboard.

(1)   Define (a) comment; (b) reserved word; (c) identifier; (d) string; (e) declaration; (f) procedure; (g) assignment operator.

(2)* Rewrite **recip.p** to use **real** rather than **integer** variables. Use the **real** division operator (/) instead of the integer division operator **div**. (You may want to refer to your Pascal book.)

(3)* The output from **recip.p** is not as attractive as it might be because of the large spaces preceding the numbers. Refer to your Pascal book to see how to format the output; then revise **recip.p** to control the spacing of the output line.

(4)* Even if you have rewritten **recip.p** to use **real** data, it may still not handle an input of zero correctly. Read your Pascal book about the **if–then** statement; then modify the **recip.p** program so that it prints the message "The reciprocal of 0 is not defined" if the user types in a zero at the prompt.

(5)* Write a Pascal program **sqroot.p** to compute the square roots of numbers entered by the user at the keyboard.

Part VIII
DOCUMENT PREPARATION

22. Document Preparation

One of the first uses for UNIX was to prepare documents for the AT&T Bell Laboratories, and document preparation continues to be one of its most important applications. In this chapter we discuss the standard UNIX text formatter **troff**, which you can use to produce attractive letters, reports, and papers.

A Brief History of UNIX Text Formatters

The first UNIX formatter was called **roff**. This is short for "run off," as in "Let's run off a copy of this." It was designed for use with simple typewriter-quality output devices such as line printers. **roff** was followed by an improved formatter called **nroff** ("new **roff**"). Still more improvements were made to produce **troff** ("typesetting **roff**"), which is designed to take advantage of high-resolution output devices such as laser printers and phototypesetters.

Formatters vs. Text Editors

A text formatter is not the same thing as a text editor, although both types of programs are often used together. On UNIX, a text editor (such as **vi**) is used to prepare a text file that can then be sent to a formatter such as **troff** to control the appearance of the output. A good formatter allows you to do such things as set the page length and margin widths, change the type font and size, control indentation, and so on.

WYSIWYG vs. Batch Formatting

Many computer systems today offer word processing programs that combine the functions of a text editor and a formatter. These programs allow you to see exactly what the final document will look like even as you type it into the file. This is sometimes called the "what-you-see-is-what-you-get" (WYSIWYG) approach to document preparation.

An alternative to WYSIWYG text formatting is the *batch method*, in which you place the formatting instructions in the same file as the unformatted text, then run the entire file through the formatter. **troff** is a batch formatter.

WYSIWYG word processors have several advantages: they are relatively easy to learn and to use, and they show you immediately how the final document will appear when it is printed. On the other hand, most WYSIWYG word processors require a sophisticated user interface, whereas a batch formatter works even with the simplest "dumb" computer terminals. Furthermore, there are some formatting problems that are best handled by the batch method.

Formatting Instructions

To use **troff**, you simply place formatting instructions in the file with the text that you want to format. There are two types of **troff** instructions. *Stand-alone* **troff** instructions occupy a complete line in the file and begin with a period (.) or an acute accent ('). For example, if **troff** comes across the following line in a text file, it inserts a space in the output:

```
.sp
```

Since regular text rarely contains lines beginning with a period, there is little danger that a stand-alone **troff** instruction will be mistaken for regular text.

In-line or *embedded* **troff** instructions are interspersed with regular text; such instructions begin with a backslash (\). For example, **troff** will print the Greek letter alpha (α) whenever it encounters the in-line instruction \ (*a. In-line instructions are often called *escape sequences*.

By the way, the special sequence of characters \ " is used to denote a *comment*. **troff** will ignore any text from the \ " to the end of that line.

Page Setup

One of the first things you should do when formatting documents with **troff** is to specify the page setup (Figure 22.1). This includes the following:

- *Page length.* This is the actual length of the paper that you are using. The default value is 11.0 inches, the standard paper size used in the United States. The page length can be changed using the **.pl** instruction.

- *Page offset.* This is the width of the left margin. The default values is 26/27 of an inch. This value can be changed by the **.po** instruction.

- *Line length.* This is the maximum length of a text line. The default is 6.0 inches. The line length is changed by the **.ll** instruction.

- *Vertical spacing.* This is the distance between single-spaced lines of text. (Double-spaced lines will be twice this far apart.) The **.vs** instruction sets the vertical spacing.

Note that you cannot set the right margin directly. Instead, the right margin is whatever is left over after the page offset and line length are set. For example, if your paper is 8.5 inches wide, and you set a page offset of 1.25 inches and a line length of 6.0 inches, the right margin will be

$$8.5 \text{ in} - 1.25 \text{ in} - 6.0 \text{ in} = 1.25 \text{ in}$$

Units of Measurement

troff employs a number of different units of measurement. For example, the **troff** instruction

```
.sp 1i
```

will cause **troff** to insert a 1-inch blank space in the output document. Similarly, the instruction

```
.sp 2.54c
```

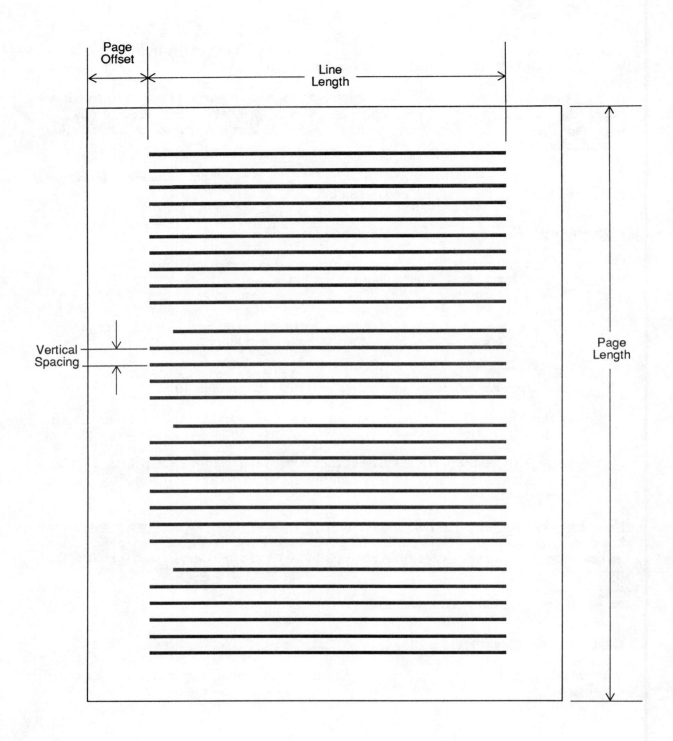

Figure 22.1. Page setup terms used by **troff**.

causes **troff** to insert a 2.54-centimeter space. The units of measurement recognized by **troff** include the following:

i	inch
c	centimeter
p	point (approx. 1/72 inch)
P	Pica (12 points, about 1/6 inch)
m	em (approximately the width of the letter "m" in the current font)
n	en (half an em)
u	basic unit (1/432 inch)
v	vertical line space

Fonts

A *font* is a set of characters all of one style and size. For example, the default font used by **troff** is 10-point Times Roman. (This text is set in 12-point Times Roman.) **troff** allows you to choose the type style using the **.ft** ("font") instruction. For instance, the following input lines

```
This text will be set in 10-point Times Roman.
.ft B      \"B stands for "bold"
This text will be set in boldface type.
.ft
This text will be set in the previous font
(10-point Times Roman).
```

would produce these output lines:

This text will be set in 10-point Times Roman.
This text will be set in boldface type.
This text will be set in the previous font (10-point Times Roman).

You can also change the font in-line using an escape sequence. For example, suppose you had the following line in your input file:

```
This shows how to \fIitalicize\fP a word.
```

troff would translate this into the output line

This shows how to *italicize* a word.

The escape sequence **\fI** changes the font to italics; **\fP** changes it back to the previous font.

Type Size

troff normally prints in 10-point type, but you can change the type size using the **.ps** ("point size") instruction. For example,

```
This will be set in 10-point Times Roman.
.ps 18
This will be set in 18-point Times Roman.
.ps
This will be set in 10-point Times Roman.
```

will produce

This will be set in 10-point Times Roman.

This will be set in 18-point Times Roman.

This will be set in 10-point Times Roman.

The actual fonts available to you may depend on your installation—ask your system administrator about this.

Filling and Adjusting

troff normally *fills* the text, which means that it takes as much of the raw input text as needed to make up a full output line. For example, consider the following text:

```
There once was a fellow named Chester,
Whose knowledge grew lesser and lesser.
It at last grew so small,
He knew nothing at all;
So they hired him as a professor.
```

troff would normally produce an output that looks something like this:

There once was a fellow named Chester, Whose knowledge grew lesser and lesser. It at last grew so small, He knew nothing at all; So they hired him as a professor.

Regardless of how the original text is broken up, **troff** takes enough of it to make up a complete output line. This obviously is not what it should do for a limerick such as this, so you would want in this case to print without filling. The **.nf** ("no fill") instruction will accomplish this:

There once was a fellow named Chester,
Whose knowledge grew lesser and lesser.
It at last grew so small,
He knew nothing at all;
So they hired him as a professor.

You can return to the fill mode using the **.fi** ("fill") instruction. When operating in the fill mode, **troff** also inserts spaces between the words to make the lines to come out flush with both margins. This is called *adjusting* or *justifying*. You can control the way **troff** adjusts the text using the **.ad** ("adjust") instruction. For example, the instruction **.ad l** ("adjust left") instruction causes the text to be flush with the left margin but ragged along the right margin.

Figure 22.2 shows some of the things you can do with the **troff** instructions we have discussed thus far.

The four blank lines above this line are produced by the **.sp 4** instruction. This text is single-spaced (using the **.ls 1** instruction). It is also filled, and right- and left-adjusted, which means that the text lines are flush with both margins. It is set in 12-point Helvetica type. The spacing between the lines is 14 points. (Remember a point is equal to 1/72 of an inch). Blahblah, blah blah & blah blah. Blah blahblah blah. Piffle.

This line is indented using the **.ti** ("temporary indent") instruction. This instruction affects only one line at a time. If you want to indent more than one line at a time, use the **in** ("indent") instruction.

This text is indented using the **.in** instruction. You may use this instruction whenever you want to indent two or more lines of text. Blahblah, blah blah & blah blah. Blah blahblah blah. Poppycock.

This text is single-spaced, filled, right- and left-justified. It is set in 12-point Times Roman type. The stand-alone **troff** instruction to select this typeface is **.ft R**. The type size is specified by the **.ps 12** ("point size 12") instruction. Blah blah blah, but blahblah & piffle, whenever blah.

The three blank lines above this line are produced by the **.sp 3** command. This text is

double-spaced (using the **.ls 2** instruction). It is also filled and right- and left-justified.

The type is 12-point Helvetica. You can select Helvetica with the **.ft H** instruction.

Blahblah, blah blah & blah blah. Blah blahblah blah. Phooey. Poppycock & piffle.

These three lines are centered
between the margins using the
.ce 3 instruction.

This text is single-spaced, filled, and left-justified, but not right-justified. To produce this effect, use the **.ad l** ("adjust left") or the **.na** ("no adjust") instruction. Either way, the text will come out with a flush left margin and a ragged right margin. Unless you specify otherwise, **troff** always adjusts both margins. (The following blank line is produced by the **.sp** instruction.)

This text is single-spaced, filled, and right-justified, but not left-justified. This means that the text is flush with the left margin, but ragged along the left margin. This effect is produced with the **.ad r** ("adjust right") instruction. Be judicious when using this format: some readers find it annoying. (The following blank line is produced by the **.sp** instruction.)

This text is single-spaced, filled, and centered by the **.ad c** ("adjust center") instruction. This leaves both the left and right margins uneven. This is not commonly done, but you may find a need for it someday. A new page is started using the **.bp** ("begin page") instruction.

Figure 22.2. Sample **troff** output (shown approximately 75% of true size).

Macros

Although **troff** is very powerful, it is not especially convenient to use. There are many things that **troff** ought to do automatically—such as creating top and bottom margins on each page, or indenting the first line of a new paragraph—which you must to tell it to do. To start a new indented paragraph, for example, you might insert the following instructions in your text file:

```
.br
.ti +5m
```

The first instruction (**.br**) causes a "break," which means it starts a new line. The second instruction (**.ti +5m**) temporarily indents the next line by 5 ems. (Remember, an "em" is approximately the width of the letter *m* in the current font.) The problem is that you would have to put these two instructions in the text file everywhere you wanted to start a new paragraph.

Most people do not use "raw" **troff** this way. Instead, they use a *macro*, which is a single instruction that replaces one or more **troff** instructions. You could define your own "paragraph" macro by putting the following lines near the beginning of your text file:

```
.de PA      \" Begin macro definition
.br         \" Start new line
.ti +5m     \" Indent 5 ems
..          \" End macro definition
```

The instruction **.de PA** stands for "define a macro named *PA*." Everything from there until the two dots (**..**) is the macro itself. With this definition, all you have to do to start a new paragraph is insert the instruction

```
.PA
```

This has the same effect as the two instructions

```
.br
.ti +5m
```

Defining a macro this way has the obvious advantage of saving you keystrokes as you prepare the text file. It is also very convenient if you later decide to change the format of your paragraphs. Suppose you wanted to change the indentation to be, say, 7 ems; instead of hunting through the entire file to change every occurrence of the **.ti** instruction, all you have to do is change the definition of the **.PA** instruction at the top of the file.

The Standard Macro Packages

Although macros can be convenient, defining your own macros can still be a lot of work. Most people prefer to use a *macro package*, which is a set of predefined macros. You will learn about the **ms** ("manuscript") macros in Chapter 24. Some of the things for which you might use a macro package instead of raw **troff** include

- *Paragraph Styles.* Using a macro package, you can choose among various paragraph styles: block, indented, quoted, etc.

- *Margins.* Raw **troff** does not automatically create margins at the top or bottom of the page, but a macro package can do this for you. (Side margins, however, are created by the **troff** page-offset instruction.)

- *Header.* A *page header* is text that is printed at the top of the page, above the main text. You can specify that a header appear on every page, or only on even or odd pages.

- *Footer.* A *footer* is text that is printed at the bottom of the page. As with headers, you can specify that a footer appear on every page, or only on even or odd pages.

- *Headings and Titles.* A macro package will allow you to place chapter and section headings in your document.

- *Displays.* A *display* is a block of text that is to be kept intact, and not split across pages.

- *Footnotes.* A macro package will handle the placement and numbering of footnotes.

Exercises

(1) Define: (a) formatter; (b) stand-alone instruction; (c) in-line instruction; (d) escape sequence; (e) point; (f) Pica; (g) em; (h) en; (i) filling; (j) adjusting; (k) font; (l) page offset; (m) macro; (n) page header; (o) footer; (p) display.

(2) What does "WYSIWYG" stand for? Are there any WYSIWYG document preparation programs on your system?

(3) How is filling different from adjusting?

(4) Standard US letter-sized paper measures 8.5 by 11 inches. In Europe, you might find a similar paper size, designated "A4," which measures 210 mm by 297 mm (approx. 8.25 by 11.75 inches). Suppose you were using A4 paper and wanted to create 1.25-inch right and left margins. What page offset and line length would you choose?

(5) The point size of type is defined (approximately) as the distance between the tops of the tallest letters (like *b, h,* or *l*) and the bottoms of the letters with descenders (like *p* and *q*). To ensure that characters on one line will not overlap characters on the lines above or below, you should set the vertical spacing to be equal to or greater than the point size. Suppose you are working with 10-point type. Express the minimum vertical spacing in (a) inches; (b) centimeters; (c) Picas; and (d) the basic **troff** unit.

23. Tutorial: Using troff

In this chapter, you will see how to use **troff** to format the letter shown in Figure 23.1.

Setting up the Page

Begin by using the **vi** editor to create a file named *chimera*:

```
$vi chimera
```

Next enter the following **troff** instructions into the file:

```
.\" Set up the page
.pl 11.0i
.po 1.0i
.ll 6.5i
.bp
.sp 1.0i
```

Before proceeding further, let's consider what these instructions do:

- `.\" Set up the page`

This is a comment line. **troff** ignores the text from the .\" to the end of the line. Note that a period is placed before the \" when the comment is on a line all by itself.

- `.pl 11.0i`

This sets the page length to 11 inches, which is standard letter size used in the United States. (If you are using different paper, put the actual page length here.)

- `.po 1.0i`

This sets the *page offset*—the width of the left margin—to 1 inch.

- `.ll 6.5i`

The *line length* instruction sets the distance from the left to the right margin. Setting the line length to 6.5 inches leaves a right margin of 1 inch (assuming you are using paper that is 8.5 inches wide.) Note that you cannot set the right margin directly—it depends on the page offset and line length.

- `.bp`

The **.bp** instruction causes **troff** to begin a new page. (It is not really necessary here.)

- `.sp 1.0i`

troff does not automatically create a head margin—you have to do this yourself with the **.sp** ("space") instruction. In this case, **troff** will create a 1-inch space.

Chimera Energy Devices

13 Mirage St., West Lafayette, IN 47906

29 February 1999

Joan Smith, President
International Widgets, Inc.
3600 Panoramic Blvd.
Berkeley, CA 94705

Dear Ms. Smith:

Last year, I ordered a set of your PerfectForm® industrial widgets for my *Mark I Perpetual-Motion Prototype*. However, after I installed the widgets, the prototype failed to achieve its energy design efficiency of 110.47%. (It also failed to produce any γ radiation.) Since I made all of the other parts myself, I conclude that your widgets were at fault, and hereby request a refund.

Sincerely,

Archimedes T. Edison
President & Director of Research

Figure 23.1. Sample **troff** letter (approximately 75% of true size).

Letterhead

Next create the fancy letterhead. Note that the name of the company ("Chimera Energy Devices") is set in 24-point Helvetica Bold type, and it is centered on the page. Use the **vi** editor to enter the following lines in the file:

```
.\" Make a fancy letterhead
.ce 2
.ps 24
.vs 28
.ft HB
Chimera Energy Devices
```

Let's examine what each of these instructions does:

- `.ce 2`

This instruction causes the next two output lines to be centered on the page. This will take care of the company name and its address.

- `.ps 24`

The **.ps** ("point size") instruction sets the type size. Remember that a *point* is 1/72 of an inch.

- `.vs 28`

The **.vs** ("vertical space") instruction sets the distance, measured in points, between single-spaced lines. As a rule of thumb, you should set the vertical spacing to be about 20% more than the point size. (In this case, that would be 28.8 points, which we round down to 28 points of vertical spacing.)

- `.ft HB`

The default type style on most systems is Times Roman (R). The stand-alone **troff** instruction **.ft** ("font") may be used to change the type style—in this case, to Helvetica Bold. Other common type styles include Times Bold (B) and Times Italic (I), Helvetica (H) and Helvetica Italic (HI), and constant-width (CW).

- `Chimera Energy Devices`

This is the first line that will be printed, in 24-point Helvetica Bold, centered between the left and right margins.

The company address is set in 16-point Times Roman type, and it is also centered on the page. To accomplish this, add these lines to your file:

```
.ps -8
.vs -9
.ft
13 Mirage St., West Lafayette, IN  47906
```

These commands add two new features:

- ```
  .ps -8
  .vs -9
  ```

These are examples of *relative* size changes. The instruction **.ps –8** reduces the type size by 8 points from its previous setting (24 points). Thus the new type size is 24 – 8 = 16 points. Similarly, the instruction **.vs –9** reduces the vertical spacing by 9 points: 28 – 9 = 19 points.

- ```
  .ft
  ```

When the **.ft** instruction is used all by itself, without an argument, it restores whatever font was in effect before the last font change. In this case, that would be the default font, Times Roman.

Printing the Page

You now have enough to print out. Write the changes into the file and quit the text editor:

$\boxed{\text{ESC}}$:wq $\boxed{\text{RET}}$

Next run your file through **troff** and redirect the output into a temporary file:

$troff chimera > chimera.tmp $\boxed{\text{RET}}$

You can now print *chimera.tmp* using **lpr** or **lp**:

$lpr chimera.tmp $\boxed{\text{RET}}$ or $lp chimera.tmp $\boxed{\text{RET}}$

If this does not work, or if it doesn't work quite right, consider the following:

(1) Your system may not have the Helvetica Bold font available. In this case, it will probably use the default font.

(2) Depending on how your particular system is set up, you may have to use the **–T** option with **troff**. For example, if yours is a PostScript (psc) printer, you might have to use the following command line to format the file:

$troff -Tpsc chimera > chimera.tmp $\boxed{\text{RET}}$

You should ask your system administrator about this.

(3) If you are using **lpr** to print the file, you may have to include the **–n** option, which indicates that the file contains formatting instructions. Thus, you would type the following command line to print the file:

$lpr -n chimera.tmp $\boxed{\text{RET}}$

Date

The next step is to produce the date.

```
.ps 12
.vs 14
.sp 4
.ti +4i
29 February 1999
```

These lines introduce some new features:

- ```
  .ps 12
  .vs 14
  ```

The rest of the letter will have a type size of 12 points, with a vertical spacing of 14 points.

- ```
  .sp 4
  ```

When the space command is followed by a number with no units of measurement, it is assumed to be the number of lines to be skipped.

- ```
  .ti +4i
  ```

The **ti** ("temporary indent") instruction changes the indentation for the next output line only. In this case, the data will be indented an additional 4 inches. We could have used an absolute measurement instead:

```
.ti 5i
```

Address and Salutation

The address block and greeting are to be printed in *no-fill mode*.

```
.nf
Joan Smith, President
International Widgets, Inc.
3600 Panoramic Blvd.
Berkeley, CA  94705
.sp 2
Dear Ms. Smith:
```

If you did not use the **.nf** command, **troff** would automatically fill the text, taking enough of each line to make up an entire output line. Consequently, most of the address block would end up on just one line.
```

Body of the Letter

For the body of the letter, you will want to fill the text. To do this, insert the instruction **.fi** to return to the fill mode. Enter the following lines:

```
.fi
Last year,
I ordered a set of your PerfectForm\(rg
industrial widgets
for my \fIMark I Perpetual-Motion Prototype\fP.
However,
after I installed the widgets,
the prototype failed to achieve its energy
design efficiency of 110.47%.
(It also failed to produce any \(*g radiation.)
Since I made all of the other parts myself,
I conclude that your widgets were at fault,
and hereby request a refund.
```

Let's look at some of the new features introduced here:

- `.fi`

The **.fi** instruction turns on the fill mode. This causes **.troff** to take as much of the input as it needs at a time to fill out an entire line. Note how the input text following this instruction is broken up. If you keep the input lines short, they will be easier to edit. When they are printed, **troff** will ignore the new lines and fill out the text properly.

- `PerfectForm\(rg`

This is an example of a **troff** in-line instruction. The escape sequence **\(rg** specifies the symbol ®. A more complete list of **troff** special escape sequences is given in Appendix D.

- `\fIMark I Perpetual-Motion Prototype\fP.`

The escape sequence **\(fI** changes the font to Times Italic; the escape sequence **\(fP** returns to the previous font.

- `\(*g`

This escape sequence specifies the Greek letter γ (gamma). A list of **troff** Greek character escape sequences is given in Appendix D.

Closing and Signature

The closing should be indented and unfilled. Add these lines to your file:

```
.in +4i
Sincerely,
.sp 3
.nf
Archimedes T. Edison
President & Director of Research
.in -4i
```

Why did we use the **.in** ("indent") instruction here, instead of the **.ti** ("temporary indent") instruction that we used before? The answer is that **.ti** only indents one line at a time, and we have several lines to indent here.

Summary

You have learned to use a number of the more important **troff** instructions, which are listed below. Note that the instructions beginning with a period (.) are stand-alone instructions, which occupy an entire input line; those beginning with a backslash (\) are in-line instructions, or escape sequences, which may be interspersed with other text.

Page Set-Up

`.pl` n	set the page length to n (default is 11.0i)
`.pl` $\pm n$	change current page length by $\pm n$
`.po` n	set page offset to n (default: 0.963i)
`.po` $\pm n$	change current page offset by $\pm n$
`.ll` n	set line length to n (default: 6.5i)
`.ll` $\pm n$	change current line length to $\pm n$
`.bp`	begin page

Spacing

`.vs` n	set the vertical space between lines to n (default: 12 points)
`.vs` $\pm n$	change current vertical spacing by $\pm n$.
`.sp`	space down a line
`.sp` n	space down n lines (or the distance specified by n)

Indentation

`.ti` n	indent the next line to n
`.ti` $\pm n$	indent the next line by $\pm n$.
`.in` n	set the indentation to n
`.in` $\pm n$	change the indentation by $\pm n$.

Font Size

`.ft` *X*	set the font to *X*
`.ft`	change to the previous font
`\f`*X*	set the font to *X*
`\fP`	change to the previous font

Type Size

`.ps` *n*	set the point size to *n*
`.ps` ±*n*	change the point size by ±*n*.
`\s`*n*	set the point size to *n*
`\s0`	change to the previous font
`\s`±*n*	change the point size by ±*n*.

Filling & Centering

`.nf`	do not fill text
`.fi`	fill text
`.ce` *n*	center the next *n* output lines

Exercises

(1)* You can double-space text using the **troff** stand-alone instruction

```
.ls 2
```

To return to single spacing, use the instruction

```
.ls 1
```

Modify your file *chimera* so that the body of the letter is double-spaced. Do you like the result?

(2)* Which fonts are available on your system? Create a file named *fonts*, and try to print text in the following fonts:

Helvetica (H)
Helvetica Bold (HB)
Helvetica Italic (HI)

Palatino (PA)
Palatino Bold (PB)
Palatino Italic (PI)

`Constant-Width  (CW)`

Some of the other fonts you might try are Courier Typewriter (CT), Techno Bold (TB), Script (SC), Century Expanded (CE), and Century Bold (CB). What happens if you request a font that is not available?

(3)* Open a file named *type.sizes*, and enter the **troff** instructions that will print the following lines:

9-point Times Roman
10-point Times Roman
12-point Times Roman
14-point Times Roman
18-point Times Roman
24-point Times Roman

(4)* Try out the **troff** special characters. Create a file named *special*, and enter the escape sequences to print these special characters:

• ° § ¢ ÷ ‡ ± ∪ ∩ ← ↑ → ↓ " " ' ' - – —

(5)* Try out some Greek characters. Open the file *special*, and add the escape sequences needed to print the following lines:

αβγδεζηθικλμνξοπρσςτυφχψω
ΑΒΓΔΕΖΗΘΙΚΛΜΝΞΟΠΡΣΤΥΦΧΨΩ

(6)* How does **spell** handle **troff** instructions? Find out by running **spell** on your file *chimera*.

24. Tutorial: Using the ms Macros

In this chapter, you will see how to use the **ms** macro package to format a text file. You will learn how to produce section headings, paragraphs, displays, footnotes, etc.

Number Registers

Use **vi** to create a file named *ms.sampler* and enter the following lines:

```
.nr PL 11.0i      \" Page length
.nr PO 1.0i       \" Page offset
.nr LL 6.5i       \" Line length
.nr PS 12         \" Point size
.nr VS 14         \" Vertical space
.nr HM 1.0i       \" Head margin
.nr FM 1.0i       \" Foot margin
```

These instructions set the values of various *number registers*, which are memory locations that control the document format. Typically, you use these registers for values that you want to apply to the document as a whole, although you can use **troff** commands to override these settings locally. Let's look at these lines one by one:

-    `.nr PL 11.0i      \" Page length`

The **.nr** ("number register") instruction is used to store values in number registers. The **PL** register controls the page length for the entire document. It can be overridden locally by the **.pl** instruction.

-    `.nr PO 1.0i       \" Page offset`

The **PO** register controls the page offset for the entire document. It can be overridden locally by the **.po** instruction.

-    `.nr LL 6.5i       \" Line length`

The **LL** register controls the line length for the entire document. It can be overridden locally by the **.ll** instruction.

-    `.nr PS 12         \" Point size`

The **PS** register controls the type size for the entire document. It can be overridden locally by the **.ps** instruction. (Do not use a *p* for "point" here—it can cause problems.)

-    `.nr VS 14         \" Vertical space`

The **VS** register controls the vertical spacing for the entire document. It can be overridden locally by the **.vs** instruction. (Do not use a *p* for "point" here—it can cause problems.)

-    `.nr HM 1.0i       \" Head margin`

The **HM** register controls the head margin. Thus, this instruction line sets a 1-inch margin at the top of each page.

-     `.nr FM 1.0i    \" Foot margin`

The **FM** register controls the foot margin. This instruction sets a 1-inch margin at the bottom of each page.

Section Headings

Our first step is to see how **ms** may be used to make numbered and unnumbered section headings. Enter the following lines into your file *ms.sampler*:

```
.NH 1
Level 1 Numbered Heading
.NH 2
Level 2 Numbered Heading
.NH 3
Level 3 Numbered Heading
.NH 1
ANOTHER LEVEL 1 HEADING
.NH 2
Another Level 2 Numbered Heading
.NH 2
Yet Another Level 2 Heading
.SH
An Unnumbered Heading
```

Write this into the file and quit the editor. Format the file with **troff** and **ms**:

```
$troff -ms ms.sampler > sample.tmp RET
```

This formats the file *ms.sampler* and puts the results into *sample.tmp*, which can then be printed in the usual way using either **lp** or **lpr**. (You can avoid creating an additional file by piping the output from **troff** directly to the print command if you wish.) When printed, the output should appear very much like that shown below:

---

1. Level 1 Numbered Heading

1.1. Level 2 Numbered Heading

1.1.1. Level 3 Numbered Heading

2. ANOTHER LEVEL 1 HEADING

2.1 Another Level 2 Numbered Heading

An Unnumbered Heading

Paragraphs

There are five basic paragraph types to choose from: conventional, left-justified, indented with tag, exdented, and quoted. Add the following lines to the bottom of your *ms.sampler* file:

```
.bp            \" Begin a page
.NH 1
PARAGRAPH FORMATS
.NH 2
Conventional Paragraph (.PP)
.PP
This shows the form of the conventional paragraph.
It is right- and left-justified,
with an indented
first line.
This kind of paragraph is produced by the \fB.PP\fP
instruction.

.NH 2
Left-Justified Paragraph (.LP)
.LP
The left-justified paragraph is similar to the
conventional paragraph,
except that its first line is
not indented.
Many fine writers prefer this form.
```

When formatted and printed, this produces the output something like that shown below.

---

3. PARAGRAPH FORMATS

3.1 Conventional Paragraph (.PP)
This shows the form of the conventional paragraph. It is right- and left-justified, with an indented first line. This kind of paragraph is produced by the **.PP** instruction.

3.2 Left-Justified Paragraph (.LP)
The left-justified paragraph is similar to the conventional paragraph, except that its first line is not indented. Many fine writers prefer this form.

Note how **ms** automatically numbers the section headings.

Next try the indented and exdented paragraph styles. Add the following lines to your ***ms.sampler*** file:

```
.NH 2
Indented Paragraph with Tag (.IP)
.IP \(bu
This is an indented paragraph with a "tag."
In this case, the tag is a bullet (\(bu).
Such paragraphs are often used to create bulleted lists.
.IP (1)
This indented paragraph uses a number for a tag.
Such paragraphs are often used to create numbered lists.
.IP
This indented paragraph has no tag.

.NH 2
Exdented Paragraph (.XP)
.XP
This is the opposite of an indented paragraph, in that
everything is indented except the first line.
This is a rarely used format.
```

Write these lines into the file and quit the editor. Format the file and print it; the output should resemble that shown below.

3.3 Indented Paragraph with Tag (.IP)

- This is an indented paragraph with a "tag." In this case, the tag is a bullet (•). Such paragraphs are often used to create bulleted lists.

(1) This indented paragraph uses a number for a tag. Such paragraphs are often used to create numbered lists.

This indented paragraph has no tag.

3.4 Exdented Paragraph (.XP)

This is the opposite of an indented paragraph, in that everything is indented except the first line. This is a rarely used format.

Finally, we try the quoted paragraph. Open your file and add these lines:

```
.NH 2
Quoted Paragraph (.QP)
.LP
The quoted paragraph is used to display a block quote
that is set off from the rest of the text.
For example,
.QP
This is an example of a quoted paragraph.
It is used to set off a long quotation.
The quoted paragraph is right- and left-adjusted
and centered between the right and left margins.
Quotations set off from the text are called
\fIblock quotations, extracts\fP, or
\fIexcerpts.\fP
.QE
```

This should produce the output shown below.

3.4 Quoted Paragraph (.QP)

The quoted paragraph is used to display a block quote that is set off from the rest of the text. For example,

> This is an example of a quoted paragraph. It is used to set off a long quotation. The quoted paragraph is right- and left-adjusted and centered between the right and left margins. Quotations set off from the text are called *block quotations, extracts,* or *excerpts.*

Note again how **ms** automatically numbers the section headings.

Displays

The quoted paragraph is appropriate for most long quotations. However, poetry is usually printed without filling, more or less centered on the page. This can be done by placing the text between the **.DS** ("display start") and **.DE** ("display end") instructions. To see how this works, place the following lines in your file:

```
.bp                   \" Begin a page
.DS B                 \" Block-centered display
My Bonnie looked into the gas tank,
The contents she wanted to see;
I lit a match to assist her:
Oh bring back my Bonnie to me!
.DE
```

The entire display text is kept together on the same page and not split across page breaks. The argument following the **.DS** instruction determines how and where the display is printed on the page. In this case, the *B* specifies a "block-centered" display. An alternative argument is *C*, which produces a centered display. Add these lines to your file:

```
.DS C                 \" Centered display
My Bonnie looked into the gas tank,
The contents she wanted to see;
I lit a match to assist her:
Oh bring back my Bonnie to me!
.DE
```

Next try the argument *I*, which produces an indented display. Add these lines to your file:

```
.DS I                 \" Indented display
My Bonnie looked into the gas tank,
The contents she wanted to see;
I lit a match to assist her:
Oh bring back my Bonnie to me!
.DE
```

The last argument to try is *L*, which produces a left-adjusted display. Add these lines to your file:

```
.DS L                 \" Left-adjusted display
My Bonnie looked into the gas tank,
The contents she wanted to see;
I lit a match to assist her:
Oh bring back my Bonnie to me!
.DE
```

Close the file, format it, and print it. The result should be something resembling the output shown below.

My Bonnie looked into the gas tank,
The contents she wanted to see;
I lit a match to assist her:
Oh bring back my Bonnie to me!

My Bonnie looked into the gas tank,
The contents she wanted to see;
I lit a match to assist her:
Oh bring back my Bonnie to me!

My Bonnie looked into the gas tank,
The contents she wanted to see;
I lit a match to assist her:
Oh bring back my Bonnie to me!

My Bonnie looked into the gas tank,
The contents she wanted to see;
I lit a match to assist her:
Oh bring back my Bonnie to me!

Summary

Page Set-Up

`.nr XX n`	set the number register *XX* to *n*
`.nr PL n`	set page length register to *n*
`.nr PO n`	set page offset register to *n*
`.nr LL n`	set line length register to *n*

Spacing and Type Size

`.nr VS n`	set the vertical spacing register to *n*
`.nr PS n`	set the point size register to *n*

Head and Foot Margins

`.nr HM n`	set the head margin to *n*
`.nr FM n`	set the foot margin to *n*

Section Headings

`.NH n`	create an *n*-level numbered section heading
`.SH`	create an unnumbered section heading

Paragraphs

`.PP`	create an indented paragraph
`.LP`	create a left-justified paragraph
`.IP tag`	create an indented paragraph with a tag *tag*
`.XP`	create an exdented paragraph
`.QP`	create a quoted paragraph

Displays

`.DS B`	begin a block-centered display
`.DS C`	begin a centered display
`.DS I`	begin an indented display
`.DS L`	begin a left-justified display
`.DE`	end a display

Footnotes

`.FS`	start a footnote
`.FE`	end the footnote
`\**`	insert a footnote mark

Exercises

(1)* **ms** allows you to insert footnotes using the **.FS** ("footnote start") and **.FE** ("footnote end") instructions. To see how this works, place these lines in your *ms.sampler* file:

```
.bp                      \" Begin a new page
.SH 1
FOOTNOTES
.LP
Footnotes\**
.FS
Like this.
.FE
are produced using the \fB.FS\fB and
\fB.FE\fP instructions.
Your footnotes will be numbered automatically.\**
.FS
Like this.
.FE
```

Write and quit the editor, then format and print the file as you did before.

(2)* A *page header* is a line of text placed at the top of each page. The header may include such items as the page number, the chapter title, the date, etc. The **.EH** ("even header") instruction produces a header on even-numbered pages, while the **.OH** ("odd header") instruction produces a header on odd-numbered pages. A header consists of three parts. Open up your *ms.sampler* file and place these lines in the file just below the point where you set the number registers:

```
.EH 'Left'Center (Even page)'Right'
.OH 'Left'Center (Odd page)'Right'
```

Print the file and note how the headers are printed on the page.

(3)* You can include the page number in your header with the percent sign (%). The date may be included by inserting the escape sequence *(DY. Modify the **.EH** and **.OH** instructions from the previous exercise like this:

```
.EH '%'ms Sample Document'\*(DY'
.OH '\*(DY'ms Sample Document'%'
```

(4)* A *page footer* is a line of text placed at the bottom of each page. The **.EF** ("even footer") and **.OF** ("odd footer") instructions produce footers on even- and odd-numbered pages, respectively. These commands work very much like the header commands. Open up your *ms.sampler* file and change the header instructions from the preceding exercise to footer instructions.

(5)* You can put a box around a word using the **.BX** ("box") instruction. For example, the line

```
.BX inside
```

produces the output

inside

Try this out for yourself. Can you use **.BX** to box more than one word at a time?

(6)* You can produce a table of contents using the **.XS**, **.XA**, **.XE**, and **.PX** instructions. The **.XS** instruction is placed at the beginning of the table, the **.XE** and **.PX** instructions at the end. The page numbers are set using the **.XA** instruction. Try this:

```
.XS xi
Preface
.XA 1
Chapter 1
.XA 7
Chapter 2
.XA 15
Chapter 3
.XE
.PX
```

25. Tutorial: Using eqn

In this chapter, you will see how to use the **eqn** preprocessor to format mathematical formulas. **eqn** can create two kinds of formulas or equations: *display* equations, which are set off from the rest of the text; and *in-line* equations, which are mixed in with regular text.

Using eqn with troff

You will need to know how to format a file using **troff** and **ms**. The command to do this has the form

```
$eqn infile | troff -ms > outfile RET
```

eqn searches through the file *infile* and formats any math formulas it finds, then pipes the results to **troff**. Next, **troff** formats the file using the **ms** macros and puts the results into *outfile*, which can then be printed in the usual way using either **lp** or **lpr**. (You can avoid creating an additional file by piping the output from **troff** directly to the print command if you wish.)

Setting up the Page

Use **vi** to create a file named *eqn.sampler* and enter the following lines:

```
.nr PL 11.0i    \" Page length
.nr PO 1.0i     \" Page offset
.nr LL 6.5i     \" Line length
.nr PS 12       \" Point size
.nr VS 14       \" Vertical space
.nr HM 1.0i     \" Head margin
.nr FM 1.0i     \" Foot margin
```

These instructions ought to be familiar—they set the **troff** number registers, just as you did in Chapter 24.

Our First Example

Add the following lines to your file *eqn.sampler*:

```
.EQ (1)
w = x + y - z
.EN
```

Write this into the file and quit the editor, then format and print the file. You should see something like this:

$$w = x + y - z \tag{1}$$

Let's examine this **eqn** specification line by line:

•   `.EQ (1)`

The **.EQ** instruction marks the start of a displayed equation. If you want the equation to be numbered, place the number after the **.EQ** instruction, on the same line. (Unfortunately, **eqn** does not automatically number the equations for you.)

•   `w = x + y - z`

This is the equation itself. Note that there are spaces between the variables in the input, but none in the output. You could produce the same result if you put extra spaces or newlines in the equation specification:

```
w =
x                +y
- z
```

If you want spaces in the output, you must specify them—you will see how in a moment.

•   `.EN`

The **.EN** instruction marks the end of a displayed equation specification.

Spacing

As we noted above, **eqn** does not insert spaces automatically—this you have to do yourself. A tilde (~) is used to created a space, while a circumflex (^) is used to specify a half-space. Let's modify the previous example to put spaces around the variables. Open the file *eqn.sampler* and add the following lines to your file:

```
.EQ (2)
w~=~x~+~y~-~z
.EN
```

Write and quit the editor, and print the file. You should see something like this:

$$w = x + y - z \qquad\qquad (2)$$

This is much more pleasing than the previous example.

Default Fonts

eqn follows the usual mathematics convention of setting variable names in italics. It sets numbers, mathematical operators, punctuation, and the following special words in Roman type:

and arc cos cosh det exp for if Im lim
ln log max min Re sin sinh tan tanh

To see how this works, enter the following lines in your file *eqn.sampler*:

```
.EQ (4)
b~=~-32^sin^A
.EN
```

Write and quit the editor, then format and print the file. You should see something like this:

$$b = -32 \sin A \qquad\qquad (4)$$

Note that the variables *b* and *A* are set in italics; everything else is set in Roman type. You can override the default settings using the **eqn** instructions **roman** and **italic**. For example, add this equation specification to your file:

```
.EQ (5)
roman b~=~italic {-32}^"sin"^roman A
.EN
```

This will produce the following output:

$$b = \textit{-32 sin } A \qquad\qquad (5)$$

There are a few interesting points to note about this formula:

- ```roman b```

This causes the variable to be printed in Roman rather than italic.

- ```italic {-32}```

Numbers and signs are normally printed in Roman type. However, you can print them in italics using the **italic** command. Note that braces {} are used here for grouping; **eqn** does not print the braces themselves.

- ```"sin"```

eqn recognizes *sin* as one of the trigonometric functions and normally prints it in Roman type. Placing double quotes around this group of characters cancels its special meaning. **eqn** then treats it as a group of variable names and prints it in italics.

Bold and Fat Characters

Often you need to set mathematical symbols in bold face. Vectors and tensors, for example, are usually set in boldface. **eqn** has two instructions that will produce bold characters: **bold** and **fat**. To see how these work, put this equation specification in your file *eqn.sampler*:

```
.EQ (6)
bold F ~=~ m bold g ~~~~~~~~~~ fat F ~=~ m fat g
.EN
```

When printed, this specification produces the output

$$\mathbf{F} = m\mathbf{g} \qquad \boldsymbol{F} = m\boldsymbol{g} \qquad\qquad (6)$$

The difference between **bold** and **fat** is simple: **bold** produces a boldface character, while **fat** produces a boldface italic character.

Special Characters

eqn allows you to specify many Greek characters and special mathematical symbols by name. To try out this feature, open up *eqn.sampler* and insert these equation specifications:

```
.EQ
Lowercase~Greek~Letters:~alpha beta gamma ... omega
.EN
.EQ
Uppercase~Greek~Letters:~\(*A \(*B GAMMA ... OMEGA
.EN
.EQ
Math~Symbols:~ >= <= != inf partial del times ...
.EN
.EQ
Special~Symbols:~ bullet cup degree dollar  ...
.EN
```

When printed, these specifications will produce the following four lines:

$$Lowercase\ Greek\ Letters:\ \alpha\beta\gamma...\omega$$

$$Uppercase\ Greek\ Letters:\ A B \Gamma...\Omega$$

$$Math\ Symbols:\ \geq\leq\neq\infty\partial\nabla\times...$$

$$Special\ Symbols:\ \bullet\cup°\$...$$

There are some interesting points to note here:

- ```
  Lowercase~Greek~Letters:~
  ```

This will be printed in italics. The tildes (~) are required to put spaces between the words.

- ```
  alpha beta gamma ... omega
  ```

eqn recognizes these as the names of Greek characters. (But don't forget to put the spaces between the words.) A complete list of these characters is given in Appendix E.

- ```
  \(*A \(*B GAMMA ... OMEGA
  ```

Many uppercase Greek letters, such as A and B, look very much like their Roman counterparts; **eqn** does not have special names for these letters. However, you can always use **troff** escape sequences for these or any other Greek letters. A complete list of the characters is given in Appendix E.

Diacritical Marks

eqn makes it easy to put various diacritical marks on variables and expressions. Try this addition to your *eqn.sampler* file:

```
.EQ
```
```

```
x bar~~~~~x dot~~~~~x dotdot~~~~~
x tilde~~~~~x hat~~~~~~x vec~~~~~~x dyad
~~~~~x under ~~~~~ { x~+~y~+~z } bar
.EN
```

This produces the output

$$\bar{x} \quad \dot{x} \quad \acute{x} \quad \tilde{x} \quad \hat{x} \quad \vec{x} \quad \ddot{x} \quad \underline{x} \quad \overline{x+y+z}$$

Note that a diacritical mark is normally applied to a single variable, but you can place a mark over multiple characters if you group them using braces.

Subscripts and Superscripts

Subscripts and superscripts may be created using the **sub** and **sup** instructions. Try this example:

```
.EQ (7)
r sup 2 ~=~
x sub 1 sup 2 ~+~
x sub 2 sup 2 ~+~
x sub 3 sup 2
.EN
```

The output produced by this specification will be something like this:

$$r^2 = x_1^2 + x_2^2 + x_3^2 \tag{7}$$

Note that when **sub** and **sup** are applied to the same variable, **sub** comes before **sup**. You get a much different result if you reverse this order. For example, the specification

```
.EQ (8)
r sup 2 ~=~
x sup 1 sub 2 ~+~
x sup 2 sub 2 ~+~
x sup 3 sub 2
.EN
```

produces the output

$$r^2 = x^{1}{}_2 + x^{2}{}_2 + x^{3}{}_2 \tag{8}$$

This certainly looks strange—**eqn** put subscripts on the superscripts rather than on the variables themselves. You can control how the subscripts and superscripts are grouped and printed by using braces. The following example shows some of the possibilities:

```
.EQ
A sub i ~~~~~
B sup n ~~~~~
C sub i sup n ~~~~~
D sup n sub i ~~~~~
E sup {nst} ~~~~~
F sub {mrz} ~~~~~
```

```
G sub { K sub N } sup s ~~~~~~
H sup { n sub i sup s} ~~~~~
I sub i sub j
.EN
```

This produces the output

$$A_i \quad B^n \quad C_i^n \quad D^{n_i} \quad E^{nst} \quad F_{mrz} \quad G^s{}_{K_N} \quad H^{n_i^s} \quad I_{i_j}$$

With complicated combinations of subscripts and superscripts, you may have to experiment.

Fractions and Derivatives

You can create fractions using the **over** instruction. Here is an example:

```
.EQ (9)
R ~=~ { rho L V } over mu
.EN
```

When formatted and printed, this specification produces the output

$$R = \frac{\rho L V}{\mu} \tag{9}$$

Note the braces; if these were removed, you would get

$$R = \rho L \frac{V}{\mu}$$

The **over** instruction is often used for derivatives. For example, the input

```
.EQ (10)
{ dy } over {dt } ~=~ {dy } over {dx } {dx } over { dt }
.EN
```

produces the output

$$\frac{dy}{dt} = \frac{dy}{dx}\frac{dx}{dt} \tag{10}$$

Here is another example that shows how to create partial derivatives with the **over** and **partial** instructions:

```
.EQ (11)
df ~=~
{ partial f } over { partial y } dy ~+~
{ partial f } over { partial x } dx
.EN
```

This produces

$$df = \frac{\partial f}{\partial y}dy + \frac{\partial f}{\partial x}dx \tag{11}$$

Brackets, Braces, and Parentheses

The previous example might look better with parentheses, but the usual parentheses would be too small. Fortunately, **eqn** will automatically scale parentheses, brackets, and braces to fit if you use the **right** and **left** instructions. To see how this is done, modify the previous specification like this:

```
.EQ (12)
df ~=~
left (
{ partial f } over { partial y }
right ) dy ~+~
left {
{ partial f } over { partial x }
right ] dx
.EN
```

This produces

$$df = \left(\frac{\partial f}{\partial y}\right)dy + \left\{\frac{\partial f}{\partial x}\right]dx \tag{12}$$

Let's examine this **eqn** specification a bit more closely:

-     `left (`

The instruction **left** tells **eqn** that you want to use grouping symbols and that they should be scaled to fit the item(s) they enclose. The opening parenthesis (tells **eqn** to use a parenthesis as the left grouping symbol.

-     `right )`

This instruction is used to close off the group with a right parenthesis. Note that every **right** instruction must have a corresponding **left**. (The reverse is not true: you may use a **left** without a **right**.)

-     `left {`

This is similar to the previous **left** instruction, except that it causes **eqn** to use a brace instead of a parenthesis. **eqn** will print a brace if it is used with **left** or **right**; in most other situations, **eqn** assumes that braces are used for grouping but are not to appear in the final output.

-     `right ]`

This instruction is used to close off the group with a square bracket. (You do not have to use the same symbol on the right as on the left of the grouping.)

The following grouping symbols may be used with **left** and **right**:

$$( ) \quad [ ] \quad \{ \} \quad \| \| \quad \lfloor \rfloor \quad \lceil \rceil$$

Piles

A *pile* is a group of symbols stacked vertically, one above the other. The **pile** and **above** instructions are used for creating piles. For example, the specification

```
.EQ
pile { 137 above { A sub i} above 22 above Z }
.EN
```

produces

$$\begin{array}{c} 137 \\ A_i \\ 22 \\ Z \end{array}$$

You can enclose the pile in parentheses or brackets using the **left** and **right** instructions. For example,

```
.EQ
left [ pile { 137 above { A sub i} above 22 above Z }
right ]
.EN
```

will produce

$$\left[\begin{array}{c} 137 \\ A_i \\ 22 \\ Z \end{array} \right]$$

Matrices

A *matrix* is a rectangular array of mathematical components. **eqn** uses the **matrix, ccol,** and **above** instructions to create matrices. Try this example:

```
.EQ
left [
matrix
{
      ccol {150 above 2 above 6}
      ccol {3 above 5 above 9}
      ccol {123 above " " above 2}
}
right ]
.EN
```

This specification will produce the following output:

$$\begin{bmatrix} 150 & 3 & 123 \\ 2 & 5 & \\ 6 & 9 & 2 \end{bmatrix}$$

Let's examine some of the interesting features introduced by this example:

- ` matrix`

The **matrix** instruction tells **eqn** that what follows is a matrix. Note that the matrix specification is enclosed by braces.

- ` ccol {150 above 2 above 6}`

The matrix is laid out column by column. Here, **ccol** tells **eqn** that this is to be a *centered column*. (You can specify a right- or left-adjusted column using the instructions **rcol** and **lcol**, respectively.) The instruction **above** shows how the elements of the matrix are placed one above the other, just as when creating a pile.

- ` ccol {123 above " " above 2}`

Note how a blank element is specified here by enclosing it in double quotes.

Integrals

The **int** instruction produces integrals. For example,

```
EQ (14)
W ~=~ int from {x = a } to {x = b} F^dx
.EN
```

The output from this specification will be

$$W = \int_{x=a}^{x=b} F \, dx \tag{14}$$

The lower limit of the integral is specified with **from**; the upper limit is specified with **to**. (You can omit either of these.)

Sums and Products

eqn lets you produce sums and products. For example,

```
EQ
sum from {i = 0} to {N} x sub i ~~~~~
prod from {i = 0} to {N} x sub i
.EN
```

The output from this specification will be

$$\sum_{i=0}^{N} x_i \qquad \prod_{i=0}^{N} x_i$$

The limits on the sum and product are specified with **from** and **to**, and either limit may be omitted.

Limits

eqn recognizes **lim** as the specification for the limit process. For example,

```
.EQ (15)
L ~=~ lim from { x -> 0} f(x)
.EN
```

lim is used with **from** but not with **to**. The output will be

$$L = \lim_{x \to 0} f(x) \qquad\qquad (15)$$

Note how we specified an arrow in this example.

Radicals

You can create radicals using the **sqrt** instruction. It is very simple to use. For example,

```
.EQ
sqrt { x sup 2 over n }
.EN
```

creates this formula:

$$\sqrt{\frac{x^2}{n}}$$

In-Line Formulas

All of the formulas we have created to this point have been displayed equations, set off from the rest of the text (if any). You can also create in-line equations, but you cannot use the **.EQ** or **.EN** to do it. Instead, you must define a pair of *delimiters*, which are symbols that tell **troff** to interpret that part of the text as a formula. Open up your file *eqn.sampler* and insert these lines:

```
.EQ
delim @@
.EN
The First Law of Thermodynamics
can be written as @DELTA E ~=~ Q ~-~ W@,
where @Q@ is the heat transferred
and @W@ is the work done.
```

This will produce the output:

The First Law of Thermodynamics can be written as $\Delta E = Q - W$, where Q is the heat transferred and W is the work done.

There are a few things to note about this **eqn** specification:

- `delim @@`

This declares @ to be the delimiter for in-line **eqn** specifications. Note that you only have to place this declaration once in your document (usually near the top). From then on, **troff** will recognize anything appearing between a pair of @ symbols as an **eqn** specification. You can use nearly any symbol as a delimiter, but avoid common symbols that you might want to use elsewhere in the document.

- `@DELTA E ~=~ Q ~-~ W@`

eqn recognizes @ as marking the beginning and end of the formula specification. It also recognizes DELTA as the name of a Greek letter. Note that you have to use tildes (~) to control spacing in the equation, just as you have to in a displayed equation.

- `@Q@`

Here again **eqn** recognizes that anything appearing between @ symbols is to be treated as an **eqn** specification. In this case, Q is set in italics.

Exercises

Practice using **eqn**. Create each of the following formulas:

$$\tan \alpha \equiv \frac{\sin \alpha}{\cos \alpha}$$

$$\Delta E = h\nu$$

$$V = \frac{4}{3}\pi r^3$$

$$6.02 \times 10^{23} \frac{\text{atoms}}{\text{mole}}$$

$$\text{r.m.s. speed} = \sqrt{\overline{u^2}}$$

$$\frac{-b \pm \sqrt{b^2 - 4ac}}{2a}$$

$$\frac{df}{dx} \equiv \lim_{h \to 0} \frac{f(x+h) - f(x)}{h}$$

$$\int_a^b f(x)\,dx \equiv \lim_{n \to \infty}\left[\sum_{i=1}^{n} f(x_i)\Delta x_i\right]$$

$$x \cdot y = |x|\,|y|\cos\theta$$

$$<x,x> = x_1^2 + x_2^2 + \cdots + x_n^2$$

$$Ax = b \;\Rightarrow\; \begin{bmatrix} a_{11} & a_{21} & a_{31} \\ a_{21} & a_{22} & a_{32} \\ a_{31} & a_{23} & a_{33} \end{bmatrix}\begin{bmatrix} x_1 \\ x_2 \\ x_3 \end{bmatrix} = \begin{bmatrix} b_1 \\ b_2 \\ b_3 \end{bmatrix}$$

26. Tutorial: Using tbl

In this chapter, you will see how to use the **tbl** preprocessor to format tables. A **tbl** specification has the following general form:

> **.TS**
> *global table attributes;*
> *table format.*
> *table text*
> **.TE**

where **.TS** and **.TE** mark the beginning and end of the table specification.

Global Table Attributes

The first line following the **.TS** instruction sets out the *global table attributes,* which govern the overall appearance of the table. Here are some of the attributes you can specify:

allbox	draw a box around each entry in the table
box	draw a box around the entire table
center	center the table between the margins
doublebox	draw a double-ruled box around the entire table
expand	make the table extend from one margin to the other
tab()	change the separator

Our first table will use the **center** attribute; we will see how to use some of the other attributes as we go along.

Table Format

The *table format* describes how many columns will be in the table, and how the entries in the columns are laid out. For example,

c	center the entries in the column
l	left-justify the entries in the column
s	allow an entry to span more than one column
n	numerical data—align decimal points

Our first example will use the **l** and **n** specifications.

Table Text

The *table text* section contains the material that will appear in the table when it is printed. This material can include words, numbers, and **eqn** specifications.

Our First Example

Use **vi** to create a file named *tbl.sampler* and enter the following lines:

```
.nr PL 11.0i    \" Page length
.nr PO 1.0i     \" Page offset
.nr LL 6.5i     \" Line length
.nr PS 12       \" Point size
.nr VS 14       \" Vertical space
.nr HM 1.0i     \" Head margin
.nr FM 1.0i     \" Foot margin
```

These instructions set the values of various number registers used by **ms** and **troff**, as you did in Chapters 24 and 25.

Next add the following lines to your *tbl.sampler* file:

```
.DS
.TS
center;
l n n.
Canada TAB 3,851,809 TAB 26,832,000
Mexico TAB 761,600 TAB 85,700,000
United States TAB 3,540,939 TAB 248,709,873
.TE
.DE
```

Write your changes into the file and quit the editor. Then format the file

```
$tbl tbl.sampler | troff -ms  > tbl.tmp RET
```

This formats the file *tbl.sampler* and puts the results into *tbl.tmp*. Print this file in the usual way using either **lp** or **lpr**. (You can avoid creating an additional file by piping the output from **troff** directly to the print command if you wish.) The output should look something like this:

Canada	3,851,809	26,832,000
Mexico	761,600	85,700,000
United States	3,540,939	248,709,873

Let's look over the **tbl** specification in more detail:

- `.DS`

This is the **ms** instruction that marks the beginning of a display. It is a good idea to set up your table specifications as displays; this prevents the tables from being split across pages.

-     `.TS`

This instruction marks the beginning of the table specification.

-     `center;`

The first line in the **tbl** specification sets the global table attributes. In this case, the entire table will be centered between the margins. Note the semicolon at the end of the line—this is required.

-     `l n n.`

This line describes the table format. In this example, there are three columns. Text placed in the first column will be left-justified (`l`). The remaining two columns will contain numbers (`n`), which will be lined up on the decimal points (or where the decimal points would be). Note that the table format ends with a period.

-     `Canada` `TAB` `3,851,809` `TAB` `26,832,000`

This is a *table text* line, which will be laid out according to the format specified by the table format. The entries are separated by tabs (although you can change this using the **tab** instruction—more about this later.)

-     `.TE`

This instruction marks the end of the table specification.

-     `.DE`

This instruction ends the display.

A More Elaborate Example

Let's modify the previous table to include column headings and a spanning table heading:

```
.DS
.TS
center, box, tab(:);
c s s
c c c
l n n.
North America
Country:Area (sq. mi.):Population
Canada:3,851,809:26,832,000
Mexico:761,600:85,700,000
United States:3,540,939:248,709,873
.TE
.DE
```

Write this into the file and quit the editor; then format and print the file. You should see something like this:

North America		
Country	Area (sq. mi.)	Population
Canada	3,851,809	26,832,000
Mexico	761,600	85,700,000
United States	3,540,939	248,709,873

This table shows some interesting new features:

- ```
  center, box, tab(:);
  ```

As before, the first line gives the global table attributes. In this case, the entire table will be centered between the margins and surrounded by a box. The **tab(:)** instruction sets the colon (:) as the item separator.

- ```
  c s s
  ```

This is the first line of the table format. It tells us that there are to be three columns, and that the first line of the table will contain a centered (c) title that may span (s) all three columns.

- ```
  c c c
  ```

The second line of the table format describes how the column headings are to be laid out—that is, centered in each column.

- ```
  l n n.
  ```

The third line of the table format gives the format of the rest of the table. As before, text placed in the first column will be left-justified (l). The remaining two columns will contain numbers (n), which will be lined up on the decimal points (or where the decimal points would be). Note that the table format ends with a period.

- ```
  North America
  ```

This is the first line of the table text. It is printed according to the first format line, that is, as a centered title spanning all three columns.

- ```
  Country:Area (sq. mi.):Population
  ```

This text line is laid out according to the second line of the table format. Adjacent entries are separated by a colon (:), which was designated as the alternate tab symbol using the **tab(:)** instruction.

- ```
  Canada:3,851,809:26,832,000
  ```

This text line, as well as the two lines that follow it, is to be laid out according to the format specified by the table format.
  ```

Vertical Lines

The table format can also be used to print vertical lines between the columns. Try this example:

```
.TS
center, box, tab(:);
c s s
c|c|c
l|n|n.
North America
Country:Area (sq. mi.):Population
Canada:3,851,809:26,832,000
Mexico:761,600:85,700,000
United States:3,540,939:248,709,873
.TE
```

This is just like the previous example, except for the vertical lines in the table format. This specification produces the following:

	North America	
Country	Area (sq. mi.)	Population
Canada	3,851,809	26,832,000
Mexico	761,600	85,700,000
United States	3,540,939	248,709,873

Font and Type Size

You can put **troff** escape sequences in your table text to control the font and type size. Open up your file *tbl.sampler* and enter these lines:

```
.TS
center, allbox, tab(:);
c s s
c c c
l n n.
.vs +2
.ps +2
\fBNorth America\fP
.ps -2
\fBCountry\fP:\fBArea\fP (sq. mi.):\fBPopulation\fP
Canada:3,851,809:26,832,000
Mexico:761,600:85,700,000
United States:3,540,939:248,709,873
.TE
```

This enlarges the main heading and prints all headings in bold. It also puts a box around each entry in the table:

North America		
Country	**Area** (sq. mi.)	**Population**
Canada	3,851,809	26,832,000
Mexico	761,600	85,700,000
United States	3,540,939	248,709,873

Let's look more closely at the changes:

* `center, allbox, tab(:);`

The **allbox** attribute causes a box to be drawn around each entry.

* `.vs +2`

This is a **troff** stand-alone instruction that increases the vertical spacing by 2 points from its current setting. This setting will be in force for the rest of the table unless changed by another **.vs** instruction.

* `.ps +2`

This **troff** stand-alone instruction increases the point size of the type by 2 points from its current setting. This will cause the table title to be printed in larger type.

* `\fBNorth America\fP`

This line shows two **troff** in-line escape sequences. The text placed between the **\fB** and **\fP** instructions is printed in bold type.

* `.ps -2`

This **troff** stand-alone instruction decreases the point size of the type by 2 points from its current setting. Consequently, the rest of the table will be printed in 12-point type.

* `\fBCountry\fP:\fBArea\fP (sq. mi.):\fBPopulation\fP`

This line causes the column headings to be printed in bold type.

Horizontal Lines

There are basically two ways to draw horizontal lines in your table. One is to place an underscore (_) for a single line, or an equals sign (=) for a double line, in the table format. Try this modification of the previous table:

```
.DS
.TS
center, box, tab(:);
c s s

_ _ _
c|c|c
= = =
l|n|n.
.vs +2
.ps +2
\fBNorth America\fP
.ps -2
\fBCountry\fP:\fBArea\fP (sq. mi.):\fBPopulation\fP
Canada:3,851,809:26,832,000
Mexico:761,600:85,700,000
United States:3,540,939:248,709,873
.TE
.DE
```

This produces the following output:

North America		
Country	Area (sq. mi.)	Population
Canada	3,851,809	26,832,000
Mexico	761,600	85,700,000
United States	3,540,939	248,709,873

You can achieve the same effect by placing the underscore and equals sign in the table text:

```
.DS
.TS
center, box, tab(:);
c s s
c|c|c
l|n|n.
.vs +2
.ps +2
\fBNorth America\fP
.ps -2

_
\fBCountry\fP:\fBArea\fP (sq. mi.):\fBPopulation\fP
=
Canada:3,851,809:26,832,000
Mexico:761,600:85,700,000
United States:3,540,939:248,709,873
.TE
.DE
```

If you want to show an underscore or equals sign in your table, you must use the **troff** escape sequences **\&_** or **\&=**.

Vertically Spanning Entries

A *vertically spanning entry* is one in which the text extends from one row down to the next row. There are two ways to specify such entries. The first uses the table format:

```
.DS
.TS
center, box, tab(:);
c s s
c|c|c
^|c|^
= = =
l|n|n
^|n|n

l|n|n
^|n|n

l|n|n
^|n|n.
.vs +2
.ps +2
\fBNorth America\fP
.ps -2
\fBCountry\fP:\fBArea\fP (sq. mi.):\fBPopulation\fP
:(sq. km.):
Canada:3,851,809:26,832,000
:9,976,186:
Mexico:761,600:85,700,000
:1,972,547:
United States:3,540,939:248,709,873
:9,171,032:
.TE
.DE
```

Format and print this. The output should look something like this:

North America		
Country	**Area** (sq. mi.) (sq. km.)	**Population**
Canada	3,851,809 9,976,186	26,832,000
Mexico	761,600 1,972,547	85,700,000
United States	3,540,939 9,171,032	248,709,873

There are some new features worthy of note here:

- `^|c|^`

This format applies to the lower part of the column headings. A carat (^) indicates that the entry in this column extends down from the row above. In this case, the labels *Country* and *Population* are centered vertically between the rows.

- `^|n|n`

Again, a carat (^) indicates that the entry spans down from the row above.

- `:9,976,186:`

This is the text line that corresponds to the previous format. The first and last entires are empty; only the middle column has an entry.

Note that the vertically spanning entries make it necessary to write a separate format line for each row of the table. This makes the table specification much longer than before.

You can produce the same table by specifying the vertically spanning entries in the table text. This tends to produce a shorter **tbl** specification:

```
.DS
.TS
center, box, tab(:);
c s s
c|c|c
l|n|n.
.vs +2
.ps +2
\fBNorth America\fP
.ps -2

\fBCountry\fP:\fBArea\fP (sq. mi.):\fBPopulation\fP
\^:(sq. km.):\^
=
Canada:3,851,809:26,832,000
\^:9,976,186:
Mexico:761,600:85,700,000
\^:1,972,547:
United States:3,540,939:248,709,873
\^:9,171,032:
.TE
.DE
```

Let's examine some of the new features introduced in this example:

- `\^:(sq. km.):\^`

A backslash followed by a carat (^) indicates that an entry extends down from the row above. In this case, the labels *Country* and *Population* are centered vertically between the rows.

- `\^:9,976,186:`

As before, a backslash followed by a carat (^) indicates that the entry spans down from the row above.

Using eqn with tbl

You can use the **eqn** preprocessor to put mathematical symbols and formulas in your table. Try this **tbl** specification:

```
.DS
.TS
center, box, tab(:), delim(@@);
c s s s
c|c|c|c.
.vs +2
.ps +1
\fBeqn\fP Symbols
.ps -1

Symbol:Name
=
@int@:int:@prod@:prod
@inter@:inter:@sum@:sum
@times@:times:@union@:union
.TE
.DE
```

The main new feature here is the **delim(@@)** attribute. This specifies that the "at" symbol (@) is to be used as an **eqn** delimiter. In other words, any text occurring between a pair of @s will be taken as an **eqn** specification.

Write this into the file and quit the editor. To format and print the file, pipe the output from **tbl** into **eqn**, then pipe the output to **troff**; finally, redirect the output into a file:

$tbl tbl.sampler | eqn | troff -ms > outfile.tmp RET

The file *outfile.tmp* can then be printed in the usual way with **lp** or **lpr**. The output should look like this:

eqn Symbols			
Symbol	Name	Symbol	Name
∫	int	∏	prod
∩	inter	Σ	sum
×	times	∪	union

Exercises

Practice using **tbl**. Make the following tables:

×		×
	O	
×	O	

eqn Symbols	
Symbol	Name
cos	cos
∫	int
∩	inter
lim	lim
×	times
∏	prod
Σ	sum
tan	tan
sin	sin
∪	union

Noble Gases			
Element	**Symbol**	**Atomic Number**	**Atomic Weight**
Helium	He	2	4.003
Neon	Ne	10	20.183
Argon	Ar	18	39.948
Krypton	Kr	36	83.80
Xenon	Xe	54	131.30
Radon	Rn	86	222

Noble Gases			
Element	**Symbol**	**Atomic Number**	**Atomic Weight**
Helium	He	2	4.003
Neon	Ne	10	20.183
Argon	Ar	18	39.948
Krypton	Kr	36	83.80
Xenon	Xe	54	131.30
Radon	Rn	86	222

Noble Gases			
Element	**Symbol**	**Atomic Number**	**Atomic Weight**
Helium	He	2	4.003
Neon	Ne	10	20.183
Argon	Ar	18	39.948
Krypton	Kr	36	83.80
Xenon	Xe	54	131.30
Radon	Rn	86	222

Noble Gases			
Element	**Symbol**	**Atomic Number**	**Atomic Weight**
Helium	He	2	4.003
Neon	Ne	10	20.183
Argon	Ar	18	39.948
Krypton	Kr	36	83.80
Xenon	Xe	54	131.30
Radon	Rn	86	222

APPENDICES

A. The UNIX Manual

The UNIX system is described in detail in a massive document called the *UNIX Programmer's Manual* or *User's Reference Manual*, or simply the *User's Manual*. Your UNIX installation may have a printed (paper) copy of this manual, or it may have an on-line (electronic) version; it may have both.

The UNIX manual has the reputation of being difficult to read. It has been said that if you can read the manual, you do not need the manual. That is a bit of an exaggeration, but the manual *is* terse and takes some getting used to. Even so, it is a good idea to get familiar with the manual—it can be very useful.

Organization of the Manual

Most UNIX manuals have eight sections:

Section 1	User Commands
Section 2	UNIX and C System Calls
Section 3	Library Calls
Section 4	Device Drivers and Special Files
Section 5	File Formats and Conventions
Section 6	Games
Section 7	Miscellany
Section 8	System Administration Command and Procedures

Your system's manuals may be arranged a bit differently. (For example, it is not uncommon to find that some spoilsport has deleted the games from the system.)

In addition to the usual eight manual sections, you may find supplementary articles and technical papers describing the UNIX system. These are usually grouped together and called something like *Documents for Use with the UNIX System*, or *UNIX User's Supplement*, or perhaps *UNIX Programmer's Manual, Volume 2*. We won't say much about this second part of the manual—if you happen to find a copy, you might want to browse through it to see if it contains anything of interest to you.

Using the man Command

If your system has an on-line manual, you can read it using the **man** command, which has the general form

    $man *command*

For example, to read the manual entry for the **cal** command, type

    $man cal RET

If your system has an on-line manual, you should see an entry similar to that shown in Figure A.1. (If you are using a printed copy, search through the manual until you find the entry for the **cal** command. It should be very similar to Figure A.1.)

```
CAL(1)                    USER COMMANDS                    CAL(1)

NAME
      cal - display a calendar

SYNOPSIS
      cal [ [ month ] year ]

DESCRIPTION
      cal displays a calendar for the specified year. If a
      month is also specified, a calendar for that month only
      is displayed. If neither is specified, a calendar for
      the present month is displayed.

      year can be between 1 and 9999. Be aware that 'cal 78'
      refers to the early Christian era, not the 20th century.
      Also, the year is always considered to start in January,
      even though this is historically naive.

      month is a number between 1 and 12.

      The calendar produced is that for England and her
      colonies.

      Try September 1752.
```

Figure A.1. The manual page for the **cal** command.

Organization of a Manual Entry

All manual entries follow much the same format. Let's examine the various parts of the entry for the **cal** command:

- CAL(1)   USER COMMANDS   CAL(1)

The first line begins and ends with the name of the command, written entirely in caps (CAL). The number in parentheses (1) gives the section of the manual in which this entry is found.

- NAME
        cal - display a calendar

The name and a one-line description of the command are listed next.

- SYNOPSIS
        cal [[**month**] **year**]

This is probably the most useful part of the **man** page. It shows how the command is actually used. Anything shown in square brackets [] is optional. In this case, the brackets show that you can use the **cal** command either by itself, with the year only, or with the month and year. Thus, each of the following commands would be legal:

```
$cal RET
$cal 1999 RET
$cal 5 1999 RET
```

- DESCRIPTION

Under this heading comes a detailed description of the command. This description may be as short as a paragraph, or it may go on for several pages.

Other Categories

The manual entry for the **cal** command is rather simple because the **cal** command itself is rather simple. Entries for other commands may contain still more headings. Depending on the command, you may see one or more of the following:

- `FILES`

Files used or created by the command are listed here under this heading.

- `SEE ALSO`

This entry will direct you to other entries in the manual that are related to the current topic.

- `DIAGNOSTICS`

Some UNIX commands generate error messages. The more important or cryptic error messages will be described under this heading.

- `BUGS`

Believe it or not, some UNIX commands contain minor errors—usually called "bugs"— that have been identified but yet not eliminated. If you are lucky, such bugs will be listed here.

Reading Longer Manual Pages

The manual entry for **cal** will probably fit entirely on your screen. Other manual entries are too long to be shown on the typical terminal screen all at once. For example, try reading the manual entry describing **man** itself:

$man man `RET`

If the entire manual entry scrolled by without stopping, you will need to use the **more** or **pg** utility:

$man man | more `RET`   or $man man | pg `RET`

The vertical line is called the *pipe symbol*. **more** and **pg** are described in Chapter 4; their use with the pipe is described in Chapter 12.

B. Access Privileges

Anything you can do to one of your own files, you can do to a file belonging to another user. Obviously, it would not be good if everyone were able to change someone else's files without permission. To prevent chaos, and to preserve privacy, UNIX allows users to restrict access to their files. To see what this means, use the **ls –l** ("list –long") command. Type

$ls -1 RET

You should see listings that look something like this:

```
drwxrwx---   2 you engr      512 Apr  1 15:53 Cal
-rw-rw----   1 you engr      997 Mar 31 10:53 fun
-rw-rw----   1 you engr      401 Mar 31 10:30 summer99
```

Let's decipher the first listing:

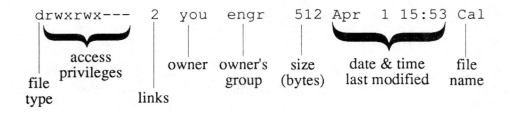

- *File type.* A *d* in the leftmost position indicates a directory. An ordinary file will have a '-' in this position.

- *Access Privileges.* These nine positions show who has permission to do what with the file or directory. More about this later.

- *Links.* A *link* is a pseudonym for a file or directory. Directory files always have at least two links, because each directory contains the hidden entry *dot* as a pseudonym for itself. Most ordinary files have just one link. You can create more links yourself, although this is beyond the scope of this book; if you are interested, see that manual entry for the **ln** command.

- *Owner.* This is the login of the person who owns the file.

- *Owner's Group.* A *group* is a collection of users to which the owner of the file belongs. (On Berkeley systems, **ls –l** does not list the group name; to see it, you have to use the **ls –lg** command.)

- *Size.* The size of the file is given in bytes.

- *Date and Time.* The date and time the file was last modified is shown here.

- *File name.* The name of the file or directory is listed last.

The nine entries showing the access permissions deserve a closer look:

```
rwxrwx---
```

Basically, there are three things that can be done to an ordinary file

r   **Read**. Examine (but not change) the contents of the file.

w   **Write**. Change the contents of a file.

x   **Execute**. If the file contains a program, run that program.

Likewise, there are three things that can be done to a directory:

r   **Read**. List the contents of the directory using the **ls** command.

w   **Write**. Change the contents of the directory by creating new files or removing existing files. (To edit an existing file requires write permission on that file.)

x   **Execute**. "Search" the directory using **ls –l**. Also, move to the directory from another directory, and copy files from the directory.

When deciding who can have access to a file, UNIX recognizes three categories of users:

- **Owner**. The owner of the file or directory.

- **Group**. Other users belonging to the user's group.

- **Public**. All other users on the system.

The first three permissions show what the owner may do; the next three show what the group may do; the last three show what the public may do. For example,

```
rwxrwx---   owner has read, write, and execute privileges
            group has read, write, and execute privileges
            public has no privileges

rw-rw----   owner has read and write privileges
            group has read and write privileges
            public has no privileges

r--r--r--   owner has read privileges only
            group has read privileges only
            public has read privileges only
```

The access privileges are sometimes called the *mode* of the file or directory. To change the mode, you use the **chmod** ("change mode") command. **chmod** uses the following notation:

u	user (owner) of the file
g	group
o	others (public)
a	all (owner, group, and public)
=	assign a permission
+	add a permission
–	remove a permission

A few examples will help you see how **chmod** is used. To give the owner execute permission without changing any other permissions, you would use

> $chmod u+x *filename* RET

Note that there are no spaces between *u* and +, or between + and *x*.

To remove read and write permissions from group members, you would use

> $chmod g-rw *filename* RET

This command will give everyone read permissions while removing any other permissions:

> $chmod a=r *filename* RET

To give everyone read and write permissions, you could use

> $chmod a=rw *filename* RET

C. The Debugger dbx

dbx can be used to debug programs written in C, FORTRAN, or Pascal. To use the debugger, you must compile your program using the **–g** option. For example, to debug the C program *recip.c*, use the command

```
$cc -g recip.c RET
```

to compile the program. Once this is done, you can run **dbx** on the executable file:

```
$dbx a.out RET
```

The computer will respond with a cryptic message (which you can ignore), something like

```
Reading symbolic information...
Read 42 symbols
```

Then it will give you a prompt that shows you are inside **dbx**:

```
(dbx)
```

Getting Help with dbx

The first thing to try is the **help** command. Type *help* at the **dbx** prompt, and press RETURN:

```
(dbx)help RET
```

The computer should respond with a listing of the various **dbx** commands:

```
Command Summary
Execution & Tracing
      catch     clear     cont      delete    ignore
      next      rerun     run       status    step
      stop      trace     when
```

and so on. Take a moment to look over the entire list. You may notice a few UNIX shell commands (**cd**, **pwd**, **setenv**, **sh**), and some other commands whose purpose you can probably guess (**edit**, for example, calls up the text editor so you can edit the source file from within **dbx**). We will not try to go over all of the available commands; you can do quite a lot with just the following dozen commands:

alias	**cont**	**display**	**help**	**print**	**quit**
run	**sh**	**step**	**stop**	**trace**	**where**

You can use the **help** command to find out more information on any of these commands. Try using **help** on itself:

```
(dbx)help help RET
```

You should see something like this:

```
help              -Print a summary of all commands
help <cmd>        -Print help about <cmd>
```

Here, <cmd> stands for any **dbx** command. This does not give a lot of information, but it is definitely better than nothing.

Running the Program

The command to run the program is, appropriately enough, **run**. Try this:

```
(dbx) run RET
```

Except for some additional information printed by **dbx** itself, your program should run as usual:

```
Running: a.out
This program calculates reciprocals.
Enter a number:
```

Enter the number *1* and press return:

```
Enter a number: 1 RET
```

The output should resemble the following:

```
The reciprocal of 1 is 1.

execution completed, exit code is 1
program exited with 1
(dbx)
```

The message "exit code is 1" simply tells you that the program completed successfully.

Running a program from inside **dbx** doesn't seem too useful—after all, it is easier to run the program directly, without first calling up the debugger to do the job. What **dbx** allows you to do is to step through the program, one line at a time, and examine the values of the variables and expressions as they change.

Listing the Source Code

The **list** command will show you the source code. Try it:

```
(dbx) list 1, 15 RET
```

This tells **dbx** that you wish to see the source code from line 1 to line 15. If your program was written in C, for example, you should see this:

```
 1     /* Compute reciprocals.*/
 2
 3     #include <stdio.h>
 4
 5     main()
 6     {
 7         int n, recip;
 8         printf("This program computes reciprocals.\n");
 9         printf("Enter a number: ");
10         scanf("%d", &n);
11         recip = 1/n;
12         printf("The reciprocal of %d is %d.\n", n, recip);
13     }
14
15
```

dbx supplies the line numbers on the left; these are not actually part of the source file.

Setting Breakpoints

A *breakpoint* is a place in the program where you want the execution to halt. Breakpoints may be set using the **stop** command. Let's set a breakpoint at line 8:

```
(dbx) stop at 8 RET
```

dbx will tell you that it has set the breakpoint:

```
stop at "recip.c":8
```

Now use the **run** command to begin execution:

```
(dbx) run RET
```

The program will run until it reaches line 8, where it will stop. **dbx** will then display line 8. For example, if you are running the C program *recip.c*, you might see

```
Running: a.out
stopped in main at line 8 in file "recip.c"
8     printf("This program calculates reciprocals.\n");
(dbx)
```

Stepping through the Program

At this point, you *could* resume execution of the program by using the **cont** ("continue") command, but it is more instructive to step through the program one line at a time. The **step** command allows you to do this. Try it:

```
(dbx) step RET
```

You should see

```
This program calculates reciprocals.
stopped in main at line 9 in file "recip.c"
9    printf("Enter a number:");
(dbx)
```

Note that the first thing you see is the line that was printed out by the previous statement. Step again, but step two lines this time:

```
(dbx) step 2 RET
```

The prompt produced by line 9 now appears:

```
Enter a number:
```

Type in a *1* and press RETURN:

```
Enter a number: 1 RET
```

The program reads in the number just as it would normally. Then it proceeds to the next line of the program and stops:

```
stopped in main at line 11 in file "recip.c"
11    recip = 1/n;
(dbx)
```

Printing Expressions

It is instructive to look at the values of the variable n. You can do this with the **print** command:

```
(dbx) print n RET
```

dbx will respond with the current value of n:

```
n = 1
(dbx)
```

Step again:

```
(dbx) print n, recip RET
stopped in main at line 12 in file "recip.c"
12    printf("The reciprocal of %d is %d.\n", n, recip);
```

Use **print** to check the values of both n and recip:

```
(dbx) print n, recip RET
n = 1
recip = 1
(dbx)
```

Use the **cont** command to continue execution of the program; this will run through the remaining lines without stopping:

```
(dbx) cont RET
```

You should see

```
The reciprocal of 1 is 1.


execution completed, exit code is 1
program exited with 1
(dbx)
```

The program is now finished running, but you are still inside **dbx**. Leave **dbx** using the **quit** command:

```
(dbx) quit (RET)
$
```

Tracing and Displaying Variables

Stepping through the program line by line and printing the variables at each step can be useful but tedious. There is a quicker way. Start up **dbx**:

```
$dbx a.out RET
```

The **dbx** prompt tells you that you are in **dbx**:

```
Reading symbolic information...
Read 42 symbols
(dbx)
```

The **display** command allows you to print the variables and their values at each stopping point. And the **trace** command causes **dbx** to step through the program line by line, without stopping. Try the **display** command first:

```
(dbx) display n, recip RET
```

You may see some messages, such as

```
n = bad data address
recip = bad data address
(dbx)
```

Next try the **trace** command:

```
(dbx) trace (RET)
```

dbx will echo the command:

```
(2) trace
```

Now run the program using the **run** command:

```
(dbx) run RET
```

dbx should run the program, line by line, displaying the values of the variables as it does:

```
Running: a.out
trace:      8      printf("This program calculates ...
n = 0
recip = 32
This program calculates reciprocals.
trace:      9      printf("Enter a number: ");
n = 0
recip = 32
trace:     10      scanf("%d", &n);
n = 0
recip = 32
Enter a number:
```

Enter the number *0* to cause an error:

```
Enter a number: 0 RET
trace:     11      recip = 1/n;
n = 0
recip = 32
program terminated by an integer divide by zero
```

Leave dbx:

```
(dbx) quit RET
```

Use the **ls** command to see that a *core* file was created:

```
$ls RET
```

You should see a *core* file. You cannot read this file, but **dbx** can. In particular, you can use the **where** command in **dbx** to find out where in the program the error occurred.

Using where

Start up **dbx** on the *a.out* file:

```
$dbx a.out (RET)
```

You might expect to see a few warnings before the **dbx** prompt appears:

```
Reading symbolic information...
warning: object file read error: text address not found
warning: object file read error: text address not found
warning: object file read error: text address not found
program terminated by an integer divide by zero
(dbx)
```

This tells you what you already know, namely that the *core* file was generated by a division by zero. The **where** command will tell you where this occurred:

    (dbx)where⌐RET⌐

```
warning: object file read error: text address not found
warning: object file read error: text address not found
warning: object file read error: text address not found
zero_divide() at 0xf773189c
main(), line 11 in "recip.c"
(dbx)
```

The last line before the **dbx** prompt tells you that the error occurred on line 11 of the function **main**.

Running Shell Commands in dbx

The **sh** command allows you to run shell commands while you are still inside **dbx**. Use this command with **rm** to delete the *core* file:

    (dbx)sh rm core⌐RET⌐

Now use **sh** and **ls** to check that the *core* file has indeed been removed:

    (dbx)sh ls⌐RET⌐

Is the *core* file still there?

Creating Aliases

Try the **help** command to see what the **alias** command does:

    (dbx)help alias⌐RET⌐

You should see a listing something like this:

```
alias                      —Print the value of all aliases
alias <newname>            -Print the value of <newname>
alias <newname> "<cmd>"  -Create an alias
```

This shows that the **alias** command may be used to (1) examine the "values" of all of the aliases already set; (2) print the value of a particular alias; or (3) create new aliases. Let's see how to create an alias for the *quit* command:

```
(dbx)alias q "quit" RET
```

Now all you have to do is type a *q* to leave the debugger:

```
(dbx)q RET
```

You can save yourself the trouble of defining aliases each time you use **dbx** by putting all of your aliases in a startup file named *.dbxinit*. Then, whenever you start **dbx**, it will look through *.dbxinit* and set the aliases it finds there.

D. troff Special Characters

Character	**troff** escape	Name	Character	**troff** escape	Name
´	\(aa	acute accent	≤	\(<=	less or equal
≈	\(~=	approx. equal	∈	\(mo	member of
~	\(ap	approximates	−	\(mi	minus
↓	\(da	arrow (down)	×	\(mu	multiply
←	\(<−	arrow (left)	≠	\(!=	not equal
→	\(−>	arrow (right)	¬	\(no	not
↑	\(ua	arrow (up)	|	\(or	or
|	\(br	box rule	∂	\(pd	partial derivative
●	\(bu	bullet	±	\(+−	plus/minus
¢	\(ct	cent sign	∝	\(pt	proportional
○	\(ci	circle	"	\` \`	quote (dbl. open)
©	\(co	copyright	"	´ ´	quote (dbl. close)
∪	\(cu	cup (union)	'	\`	quote (open)
†	\(dg	dagger	'	´	quote (close)
≡	\(==	defined as	®	\(rg	registered
°	\(de	degree	⊂	\(sb	subset
‡	\(dd	double dagger	⊆	\(ib	subset (improper)
—	\(em	em dash	⊃	\(sp	superset
∅	\(es	empty set	⊇	\(ip	superset (improper)
∇	\(gr	gradient	□	\(sq	square
`	\(ga	grave accent	√	\(sr	square root
≥	\(>=	greater or equal	¼	\(14	one quarter
∞	\(if	infinity	½	\(12	one half
∫	\(is	integral sign	¾	\(34	three quarters
∩	\(ca	intersection			

Special Characters in **troff**

Greek Characters in **troff**			
Character	**troff** escape	Character	**troff** escape
α	\ (*a	Α	\ (*A
β	\ (*b	Β	\ (*B
γ	\ (*g	Γ	\ (*G
δ	\ (*d	Δ	\ (*D
ε	\ (*e	Ε	\ (*E
ζ	\ (*z	Ζ	\ (*Z
η	\ (*y	Η	\ (*Y
θ	\ (*h	Θ	\ (*H
ι	\ (*i	Ι	\ (*I
κ	\ (*k	Κ	\ (*K
λ	\ (*l	Λ	\ (*L
μ	\ (*m	Μ	\ (*M
ν	\ (*n	Ν	\ (*N
ξ	\ (*c	Ξ	\ (*C
ο	\ (*o	Ο	\ (*O
π	\ (*p	Π	\ (*P
ρ	\ (*r	Ρ	\ (*R
σ	\ (*s	Σ	\ (*S
ς	\ (ts		
τ	\ (*t	Τ	\ (*T
υ	\ (*u	Υ	\ (*U
φ	\ (*f	Φ	\ (*F
χ	\ (*x	Χ	\ (*X
ψ	\ (*q	Ψ	\ (*Q
ω	\ (*w	Ω	\ (*W

E. eqn Special Characters

Mathematical Symbols in **eqn**			
Symbol	**eqn** designation	Symbol	**eqn** designation
≈	approx	×	times
·	cdot	∪	union
∇	del	→	->
$	dollar	←	<-
∇	grad	≡	==
½	half	≥	>=
∞	inf	≤	<=
∫	int	≠	!=
∩	inter	≪	<<
	nothing	≫	>>
∂	partial	· · ·	...
′	prime	, . . . ,	,...,
Π	prod	±	+-
Σ	sum		

Greek Characters in **troff** and **eqn**					
Character	**troff** escape	**eqn** name	Character	**troff** escape	**eqn** name
α	\(*a	alpha	Α	\(*A	
β	\(*b	beta	Β	\(*B	
γ	\(*g	gamma	Γ	\(*G	GAMMA
δ	\(*d	delta	Δ	\(*D	DELTA
ε	\(*e	epsilon	Ε	\(*E	
ζ	\(*z	zeta	Ζ	\(*Z	
η	\(*y	eta	Η	\(*Y	ETA
θ	\(*h	theta	Θ	\(*H	THETA
ι	\(*i	iota	Ι	\(*I	
κ	\(*k	kappa	Κ	\(*K	
λ	\(*l	lambda	Λ	\(*L	LAMBDA
μ	\(*m	mu	Μ	\(*M	
ν	\(*n	nu	Ν	\(*N	
ξ	\(*c	xi	Ξ	\(*C	XI
ο	\(*o	omicron	Ο	\(*O	
π	\(*p	pi	Π	\(*P	PI
ρ	\(*r	rho	Ρ	\(*R	
σ	\(*s	sigma	Σ	\(*S	SIGMA
ς	\(ts				
τ	\(*t	tau	Τ	\(*T	
υ	\(*u	upsilon	Υ	\(*U	UPSILON
φ	\(*f	phi	Φ	\(*F	PHI
χ	\(*x	chi	Χ	\(*X	
ψ	\(*q	psi	Ψ	\(*Q	PSI
ω	\(*w	omega	Ω	\(*W	OMEGA

INDEX